Childhood in Generational Perspective

The Bedford Way Papers Series

Childhood in Generational Perspective

Edited by
Berry Mayall and Helga Zeiher

Bedford Way Papers

**INSTITUTE OF
EDUCATION**
UNIVERSITY OF LONDON

First published in 2003 by the Institute of Education, University of London,
20 Bedford Way, London WC1H 0AL
www.ioe.ac.uk

Over 100 years of excellence in education

British Library Cataloguing in Publication Data:
A catalogue record for this publication is available from the British Library

ISBN 0 85473 689 1

Design and typography by Joan Rose
Cover design by Andrew Chapman

Typeset by Alden Books

Printed in Europe by the Alden Group, Oxford

Contents

List of authors

Leena Alanen is Professor and Head of the Department of Early Childhood Education, University of Jyväskylä, Finland.

Peter Büchner is Professor of the Sociology of Education, Institute of Education, Marburg University, Germany.

Pia Christensen is Senior Researcher at the National Institute of Public Health, Copenhagen University, Denmark.

Michael Corsten is Senior Researcher and private lecturer at the Institute for Sociology, Jena University, Germany.

Heinz Hengst is Professor of Social and Cultural Sciences at the Hochschule, Bremen, and member of the Institut für Popular- und Kinderkultur at Bremen University, Germany.

Berry Mayall is Professor of Childhood Studies at the Social Science Research Unit, Institute of Education, London University, England.

Alan Prout is Professor of Sociology in the Department of Applied Social Science, Stirling University, Scotland.

Helga Zeiher was a researcher for many years at the Max Planck Institute for Human Development in Berlin. She retired in May 2002 but continues to work on research projects.

Foreword: The legacy of Karl Mannheim

I am delighted to see the work of Karl Mannheim being used as one of the key conceptual points of departure for this book on the sociology of childhood and particularly pleased that such a volume is being published by the Institute of Education. As a former Karl Mannheim Professor of Sociology of Education at the Institute, I have often felt that the continuing importance of Mannheim's work, and especially that on the theme of 'generation', has been underestimated.

Karl Mannheim was born into a middle-class Jewish family in Hungary at the end of the nineteenth century. After gaining his doctorate in philosophy at the University of Budapest in 1918, he fell foul of the new counter-revolutionary government in Budapest and left for Vienna in December 1919. From there, he moved to Germany where many of his most formative intellectual experiences took place in exile under the Weimar Republic. He went initially to Freiburg and Berlin but settled in Heidelberg. In 1930, Mannheim became professor of sociology and head of the newly created College of Sociology at the University of Frankfurt. In 1933, he was removed by the Nazis from his position in Frankfurt and came, via Amsterdam, to England where he held a temporary position in sociology at the London School of Economics and lectured in the sociology of education at this Institute. In 1946 he took up a chair of education at the Institute, just a year before his untimely death at the age of 53.

As I observed in a lecture I delivered on the 50th anniversary of his death, although Mannheim's work on the sociology of knowledge is still cited in some fields of sociology, much of his work has been relatively neglected in recent years (Whitty 1997). His theoretical work on the sociology of knowledge was unfashionable among Marxist sociologists of education in the 1970s, partly because he resisted the notion that all ideas could be understood in terms of relations of class. But, notwithstanding the unremitting maleness of his language, one might have expected him to be cited more by feminist writers, since – unusually among male sociologists of his era (and since?) – he had pointed out that women's interests were not best served by constantly having their voices mediated by men. And, insofar as he generalised this argument to other social groups, it might be thought surprising that his work was not taken up in the 1980s and 1990s by postmodern and post-structuralist writers.

Certainly, his discussion of the growth of 'social techniques' which penetrate deep into our private lives and subject 'to public control psychological processes which were formerly considered as purely personal' in some ways anticipates later Foucauldian concerns with 'moral technologies'. But while some of his discussions of consciousness and awareness do anticipate contemporary notions of reflexivity, it would actually be extremely difficult to characterise Mannheim as a post-structural or postmodern theorist by any stretch of the imagination. His social psychology of personality was at odds with the notion of the decentered subject and the various 'solutions' he sought and provided to the 'problem' of relativism retain little currency today. His work was also firmly set in the redemptive project of the Enlightenment.

Yet some of the themes he addressed are surprisingly contemporary, or at least relate to issues that continue to concern us, both in sociology and in education. Like Mannheim, many contemporary social theorists still struggle with the prospect of losing any basis for claiming the superiority of one account over another – and continue to seek a viable epistemological basis for social science and social intervention. To put it in contemporary terms, rather than those of his own times, Mannheim sought a way of accepting the critique of essentialism and foundationalism without being disempowered in the process.

His particular way of doing that was rather less appropriate. Jean Floud, who knew Mannheim in the 1930s and was herself later Reader in the sociology of education at the Institute, suggests that by the 1940s Mannheim 'had turned from the fine points of the diagnosis [of the social crisis of the times] to the active political problem of controlling the descent into disaster' (page 49). Indeed, with the hindsight of the late 1950s, Floud poured scorn on Mannheim's 'joyful conviction that Sociology, the science of social action, can banish or mitigate the horrors of social change' (Floud 1959: 42).

Nevertheless, the contributions brought together here show that, whatever reservations one may have about the direction of some of Mannheim's later writings, aspects of his work can still be a fertile source of concepts for social scientific analysis today. In particular, this collection shows that his work on generation, and his concept of 'generational unit', maintains its power to help us think through contemporary issues in the sociology of childhood. And, even beyond that, as his intellectual biographer puts it: 'if many of his answers can be rejected, the questions he raised ... cannot' (Loader, 1985: 189).

Geoff Whitty
Director
Institute of Education

References

Floud, J. (1959) 'Karl Mannheim'. In A.V. Judges (ed), *The Function of Teaching*. London: Faber and Faber.

Loader, C. (1985) *The Intellectual Development of Karl Mannheim*. Cambridge: Cambridge University Press.

Whitty, G. (1997) *Social Theory and Education Policy: The legacy of Karl Mannheim*. London: Institute of Education.

Introduction

Berry Mayall and Helga Zeiher

The sociology of childhood has been developed for more than 20 years, since the early 1980s. An important motive for developing this new discipline was scholars' dissatisfaction with previous branches of sociology, which understood children only as objects of socialisation. Purpose and shape was given to this enterprise through the work of a group of scholars, including Jens Qvortrup and Helmut Wintersberger, at the European Centre for Social Welfare Policy and Research in Vienna. Perhaps the first paper readily available to UK readers was 'Placing children in the division of labour' (Qvortrup 1985). Noting that psychologists stress individual development and childhood as a transitional phase, Jens Qvortrup argued that attention should also be paid to the positioning and forming of childhood in society and to children's life as children: 'From a dynamic point of view it is not the individual's passage through childhood into adulthood which calls for attention, but the changes and continuities of a persistent age-group' (Qvortrup 1985: 133).

In the late 1980s the same group of scholars organised a 16-nation programme of research under the title 'Childhood as a Social Phenomenon' (1987–92) which aimed to study, at macro level, socio-economic and legal factors structuring childhood. Of particular interest was the generational perspective, since 'power, resources and rights are unevenly distributed between children and adults. The dynamic relationship between generations at the social macro level is one of the project's core perspectives' (Qvortrup 1991: 17).

Generation was thus identified early on as a key concept for the sociological study of childhood. Students' attention was drawn to the social processes which at any one time construct childhood in certain ways, and also to interrelations between those who inhabit the social categories of childhood and adulthood. 'Construction', as Leena Alanen formulates in Chapter 1, involves agency, and, it can be argued, the agency of both adults and children, who through processes of relational practice construct adulthoods and childhoods; she has called such processes 'generationing' (Alanen 2001: 129). In this argument, the sociology of childhood, through consideration of generation, has to take account of both structure and agency – and their intersections and relative power.

The idea for this book developed out of some earlier work, in which a number of researchers had collaborated to consider common ground in issues arising from our empirical studies. Through a series of meetings, we had focused our attention on generation as a concept that might help us understand child-adult relations as exemplified in our data (Alanen and Mayall 2001). In order to focus explicitly on generation, we had to look for and reflect on how the term is used in current sociology. We found ourselves confronted with widely varying concepts and sociological traditions. It seemed especially challenging to consider relations between our concept of generation – formed by the above-mentioned social-structural childhood socio-logy – and socio-cultural generation concepts, and so we began to revisit the work of Karl Mannheim,[1] whose essay 'The problem of generations' (1952 [1928]) was basic in the development of this strand of sociological study. In 2001, we held an international meeting in London to which some German scholars were invited, since in Germany the tradition of Mannheim's thinking seemed to be more lively than in the UK, and these scholars had explicitly worked on generational issues.

Hence this book does not present and discuss all the concepts of generation used in childhood sociology. Rather it has a certain focus within this arena; it is a book on the possible impacts of Mannheim's theory of historically located generations on the sociology of childhood. The aim of this book is to reflect on how far his concept of generations is useful within childhood sociology, and on the advantages of bringing together the differing concepts.

Differing concepts of generation

One (time-honoured) starting point is dictionary definitions. The Oxford English Dictionary (1989 edition) gives a number of definitions of generation:

> I. The action of generating. 1. The act or process of generating or begetting physically; procreation; propagation of species. 2. Production by natural or artificial processes (as of plants, animals, substances etc).
>
> II. That which is generated. 3. Offspring, progeny. 4. Offspring of the same parent or parents. 5. The whole body of individuals born about the same period; also the time covered by the lives of these. 6. Family, breed, race; class, kind or 'set' of persons.

These definitions carry ideas about time and change and about relations. The first main group defines the action of generating, a meaning used as far back as the fourteenth century. The second main group draws our attention to two main categories: children in kinship relation to parents, and the notion of a social group, born at about the same time. For our purposes, the step from the kinship level (3 and 4) to the societal level (5) is of central interest. As a societal development, such a step took place when society shifted to modernity. A generalisation from personal kinship relations to societal relations happened in two different arenas, each creating another not-kinship notion of generation – the socio-cultural arena and the socio-structural arena.

In the socio-cultural arena, personal kinship relations were generalised into relations between generation groups in society.

When modernity brought about the speeding up of social change not only in the realm of economics and technology but also in politics and culture, 'new' generations showed that they had attitudes and cultural identities in common which were different from those held by the preceding generation of their parents. Such a generation group includes not only the people who live at a time at the same kinship stage in a family (all sisters and brothers) but also all people born at about the same time: that is, 'sisters' and 'brothers' not in a particular family but in the wide realm of a society.

This kind of generalised generation concept was developed at the beginning of the twentieth century, first in the history of art (Pinder 1926). Karl Mannheim transported the idea into the realm of societal and political ideas and perceptions. Within the sociology of knowledge ('Wissenssoziologie'), Mannheim (1952 [1928]) was interested in the interrelations between ideas about reality, and social structures and processes. Aiming not only – as in the Marxist tradition – to focus on interrelations between ideologies and social class positions, Mannheim wanted to understand how ideas and concepts are rooted in the social experiences which people born in the same period have in the particular historical situation when they are young, and what makes these people into a coherent group. In analogy to the concept of social class positions he formulated a concept of the historical location of generations (generation groups) in society. He called those people a generation, whose way of thinking and of perceiving social reality had developed in a way that is based on common experiences early in their lives.

Mannheim distinguished three differing levels of togetherness. People born at a certain time are exposed to certain sets of social events and ideas; they share a generational 'location'. They, or some of them, may also develop a shared interpretation of experiences; they become an 'actual generation'. Thirdly, they may form a 'generational unit', which associates and even works together with common ideas and goals. (For fuller description and discussion, see Chapter 2.) Mannheim defines each generation as a unique group of people born in the same period and region and becoming older together. They belong to their generation throughout their life.

In the socio-structural arena, when important component parts of the dependency relations between kinship generations were reorganised at societal level by the state, personal kinship relations were generalised into generation positions and structures of childhood and adulthood which are opposed within the generational order of society. Such processes were the institutionalisation of children's education in the compulsory school system, and the institutionalisation of material provision for the elderly in the state pension system. These 'generations' are permanent social structures which are opposed by their interdependencies and by more or less unequal power relations and distribution of resources. This is comparable to the opposition of women's and men's positions in the societal gender order. Each of these 'generations' is inhabited by people of a specific age group. In the course of their life, individuals shift from one generational position to the next when they become older, and their former positions become inhabited by other people. Childhood becomes inhabited by newborn children (Qvortrup 1994: 23).

In the development of both kinds of generalised concepts of generation in sociology, a special attention towards young age can be noted. In the socio-cultural arena, where people born in the same period and thinking in a common way are looked at as a generation group, this is due to the ways in which learning processes are understood. In so far as learning in early life is considered to be most important for the formation of socio-cultural consciousness and identity, investigators of such generations look thoroughly at what happens when people are young. Mannheim's implicit learning theory emphasised the predominance of experiences in early life. As he was particularly interested in political thinking, he considered 'youth' to be the youngest group in society who will be impressed by political events and situations in their own particular way. Furthermore, Mannheim's emphasis on youth cannot be understood without noting that he formulated it in a period when youth was given high importance in German society. At the beginning of the twentieth century the 'youth movement' was very strong in Germany; 'youth' had become a myth associated with hope for social renewal and progress. Mannheim's generation theory has to be seen as part of the theorising that accompanied and followed this social movement.

Today a social movement for children has become strong; we take children seriously in their agency as members of society, and therefore we may argue that the formation of generations should be seen as beginning in childhood. We should look for and study childhood generations, too.

In the socio-structural arena, the position of childhood in the generational order has been emphasised in the last two decades. Certainly this is due to children's less powerful and minor position, as is evidenced in low birth rates, in children's relatively high poverty rates, and in their lack of political participation. It may be said that socio-structural childhood sociology emerged when these problems became obvious in European societies. In recent years the generational order of society has been further brought into discussion because of demographic developments at the other end of the lifespan. A sociology of old age is now emerging and, together with childhood sociology, allows for analysis of the whole generational construction of society.

Generation-related studies have been undertaken with differing emphases in Germany and the UK. Differences are certainly due to the particularities of social and political developments in each country during the twentieth century, and to differing issues and concepts in social sciences. It is certainly not by chance that Mannheim formulated his theory of generations in Germany and that his concept received much attention in that country.

In Germany, within the socio-structural arena, the system of generational relations has been the subject of theorising and research since the late 1970s because of political problems centring on the appropriate division of childcare provision between the family and the state. In recent years children's accelerating rate of relative poverty as well as demographic developments has led to more research and sociological debates on the generational order of German society (Kränzl-Nagl, Mierendorff and Olk 2003). In family and in education sociology, the financial, practical and cultural transfers between family generations are being studied (see Chapter 3). In this debate, as documented in several collections of papers (Lüscher and Schultheis 1993; Liebau and Wulf 1996; Mansel, Rosenthal and Tölke 1997; Ecarius 1998; Kohli and Szydlik 2000), the distinction made by Franz-Xaver Kaufmann (1993) between generation relationships ('Generationenbeziehungen') on the personal level and generation relations ('Generationenverhältnisse') at societal levels has been shown to be useful.

In the socio-cultural arena, a strong tradition of identifying youth generations has characterised German youth sociology[2] since the 1920s – at Mannheim's time, when differences between youth generations before and after the political and cultural break and upheavals at the end of the First World War were strongly evident. That break and the equally sharp break at the end of the Second World War stimulated social scientists as well as journalists to describe how differing generations were involved and formed. The after-war youth in the 1950s was characterised by the sociologist Helmut Schelsky (1957) as 'the sceptical generation'; later the term '1968 generation' was used not only to describe the anti-authoritarian groups in existence at that time but, frequently, to represent the self-identity of social groups and birth cohorts who were not directly involved in the students' rebellion. Later still, a new youth generation was seen as related to the peace and ecology movements; and from then on it has become popular in newspapers to identify more and more young 'generations', to characterise and label them through features related to consumerism and media-related lifestyles.

In the United Kingdom, generation has not been an important concept in childhood sociology. In terms of Leena Alanen's three sociologies of childhood (see Chapter 1, page 28) – the sociology of children, deconstructive sociologies of childhood, and the structural sociology of childhood – the first two have predominated in the UK. As Leena Alanen says, it is only in the third that generation becomes an explicit theoretical concern. Traditionally, social constructionism has been an important strand of thought in UK work. A starting point was critiques of developmental psychology, which argued that much of it is just codification of current western concepts of childhood (for example, Skolnick 1975; May and Strong 1980; Bradley 1989). The notion that concepts of childhood vary across societies and across time has been pursued through comparison of texts by key thinkers, such as Locke and Rousseau (Kessen 1965; Jenks 1982) and through study of the impact on sociological thought of dominant social thinkers, such as Parsons and Piaget (Jenks 1996: Chapter 1). UK historians have set out striking accounts of variations in models of childhoods across time (Cunningham 1991; Hendrick 1994). It would probably be fair to say that the collection of papers *Constructing and Reconstructing Childhood*, edited by James and Prout (1997 [1990]), has been highly influential in giving value, as its title suggests, to social constructionism in childhood studies.

Important within this paradigm has been the child as social actor. Much UK sociological work on children and childhood has taken place within the sociology of children. It has focused on the local, on children as active in constructing their own childhoods, or their own lives. (It is of course easy to identify children as social actors, since children themselves display clear evidence of their activity and agency.) Indeed, in the Economic and Social Research Council's recent research programme, Children 5–16 (1995–2001), with its stated emphasis on the child as social actor, most of the 22 projects studied children's agency, and explicitly worked both 'with' and 'for' children (Prout 2002). Working 'for' children is an important theme in the UK social research scene, with emphasis on the rights and more often the wrongs of children and childhood. This may be accounted for by UK social policies on towards childhood. It is not only that the last 20 years of the twentieth century saw huge increases in rates of child poverty (from 10 per cent to 30 per cent) and its attendant ills; it is also that, although the UK government ratified the UN Convention on the Rights of the Child (CRC) in 1991, UK governments since then have done relatively little to implement it, compared to some of our European neighbours. There are thus good and pressing reasons for researchers to investigate the extent to which children's rights are respected, in part through asking children themselves about their experiences and understandings. In sum, most sociological research in the UK, to date, has therefore fitted within 'the social construction of childhood' and 'the sociology of children' rather than within structural sociologies.

We must also note the importance of academic institutions in forefronting, and even controlling, some research and teaching areas. In the UK, children have belonged to developmental psychology, which remains the dominant discipline. There are still few academic departments offering 'childhood studies' and (as far as we know) most of these assign high value to psychological approaches and to welfarist concerns. Furthermore, the long and continuing tradition of youth studies in the UK, and the pervasive idea that youth or 'adolescence' is the key period when personal, social and political identity is formed (as also in Mannheim) has left little theoretical space for the view that childhood may (also) be a key period in such identity formation. As in Germany, there has been some emphasis on youth identities changing between generation groups in response to social influences – we have, for instance, the 1968 generation, and 'Thatcher's children' (Pilcher and Wagg 1996). But in our stratified and patriarchal society, scholars in youth studies have been concerned with the labelling of some youth groups as social problems and, accordingly, have seen social class, gender and ethnicity as key concepts.

However, the UK version of the sociology of childhood has benefited from international networks, collaborations and conferences. And there are some indications that more structural concepts may take their place alongside the sociology of children and deconstructive sociologies; that generation may be rising up the conceptual agenda in the UK. One impetus is the increasing respect for the idea that childhood is relational with adulthood; that childhood has to be understood in its distinctiveness from adulthood; and that processes in child-adult relations are central to understanding the lives and experiences of children (for example, Alanen and Mayall 2001; Mayall 2002). Thus the notion of a generational order makes its appearance. Research in other areas may also lead to increased interest in generation. The establishment of gerontology has drawn renewed attention to generation groups, and how the experience and concepts of cohorts of older people may vary, depending on when – in social history – they were born and grew up and became 'old' (for discussion see Edmunds and Turner 2002: 1–5). That people live longer and are active longer is leading to consideration of inter-generational issues – the contributions grandparents make to their grown-up children and to their grandchildren in kind, in work, in care (Brannen and Moss 2002). Feminist work is drawing attention to the changing social status of women across the generations (Pilcher 1994).

Recently another impetus for studying generation has arisen out of dissatisfaction with the concept of social class as the key to understanding change. Edmunds and Turner (2002) argue that generation provides a more important key for understanding the twentieth century. A generation, they say, can be defined in terms of a collective response to a traumatic event or catastrophe, and may include individuals born later who identify with an earlier generation (for instance, the 1968 generation). The authors focus first on youth movements, then on developments in UK, French and US intellectual thought – highlighting the importance of war, occupation and migration in producing intellectual generations. In particular, they argue that migrants and women have played important parts in challenging and changing dominant traditional concepts of national consciousness. In focusing on the influences of migrants and women, Edmunds and Turner raise interesting issues. In their focus on youth and adults, they follow traditional patterns of thought, wherein children are not understood as active contributors, but are excluded from consideration, as inhabiting a pre-social domain.

Interconnecting both generation concepts

In this book, we present a range of perspectives but, as mentioned above, we do not cover all generation and generation-related concepts that are important in recent sociology. Thinking about the impact of Mannheim's theory has led us to emphasise a socio-cultural approach to generation. Yet it is the aim of this book to point to problems that are best studied across the socio-cultural and socio-structural arenas: generation groups of people born at about the same time and generation structures in the generational order of the society. While we consider work within each of the two arenas to be necessary, we would also emphasise the importance of crossing the borders between them and of relating the concepts wherever the problem under consideration requires this, thereby paying attention to the different approaches without mixing up or confusing them. We argue for the advantage of combining both approaches by looking for the special historical shape of each of the birth cohorts that at any one time are interacting as adults and children, and constructing their intergenerational relationships and generational relations. Therefore in this book we do not present 'pure' socio-structural research or biographical research on features of particular socio-cultural generations. Instead the chapters of this book discuss issues as follows.

Processes of producing generation – theoretical frameworks
Leena Alanen starts by distinguishing three strands of sociological work on children and childhood. She describes firstly the 'sociology of children' approach, where children as social actors are studied – their experiences, views, actions and relationships. Knowledge of these is seen as valuable in its own right. Secondly,

she identifies a social constructionist approach, where the focus is on models of childhood and how and why they differ and change; thirdly, she pinpoints structural approaches which understand childhood as a permanent component of the social structure, or social order. It is here that generation becomes a specific concern, for it identifies the social structure that makes children as a group different from other groups.

Leena Alanen then considers theoretical aspects of how the Mannheimian generation theory could be related to childhood sociology. She argues that Mannheim did not conceptualise his 'generation' as an independent variable, or pervasive social cause that can have implications for many social phenomena. Rather he saw it as a dependent variable, brought about or structured by a number of socio-cultural factors or events.

How to study or analyse this 'bringing about' is the next question. Leena Alanen proposes an approach based on relational thinking. She distinguishes between 'categorical' analysis, where categories of people – such as men and women in gender analysis – are taken for granted and empirical relations between them are described; and processual analysis, which studies the processes whereby categories such as gender are constituted. The first may be understood as concerning external relations; the second internal relations. She argues for the relevance, certainly in childhood studies, of studying these processes, and contends that this entails recognising agency – the agency of both children and adults. The two generational categories of children and of adults are thus found to be 'recurrently produced' through relational practices. It is important to stress that this understanding of child participation is not restricted to the idea of child as social actor, but considers child agency in the context of larger social structures: that is, for instance, it considers child power, or lack of power, to influence events and other people.

Michael Corsten's analysis of the concept of 'generation' is in the Mannheimian tradition. The central questions of his paper are: How do generations emerge? How does coherence of generation and a collective identity come about? And, nowadays, does it make 'sense at all to talk about collective identity'? Taking into account the social tendency towards individualisation, from the individual's point of view the answer to the last question could be no, since people refer symbolic meanings to their own individual person and not to their being a member of a collective. Yet Michael Corsten argues that the coherence of a generation through its sense of collective identity is generated – even as a 'weak tie' – by the 'social structuring of time and of time perspectives'.

After giving an overview of how Mannheim conceptualised the coherence of a generation, and of differing strands of research beyond Mannheim, Michael Corsten discusses if and how, in the age of adolescence, a collective feeling of belonging to a generation group may be produced. Firstly, in our society's 'objective timetable' of the lifecourse, youth is commonly seen as a phase which is an important precondition to becoming an autonomous person, and this challenge has to be overcome in the same historical time by the young people who make up an age cohort. Even if this is done through a variety of intra-generational differentiations, young people of the same cohort share the discursive processes by which a 'collective generational background' is created. The second time aspect is what Michael Corsten calls the dramatic time perspective. Not only is the order in which events and experiences follow each other in the biography significant; it is also important to understand that 'later biographical experiences work as revisions of the former ones'. The third is the formation time of a generation, understood as the process of emergence of 'a common horizon of a shared discourse of symbolic distinctions' as well as – from the point of view of an already established generation – the generation's own perspective on 'when we were young together'. Thus Michael Corsten conceptualises identity as a process of 'the contingent turns/attempts of self-identification' and of 'biographical revisions', and asks whether this process should be considered as beginning in childhood.

Intergenerational relations – in and beyond the family
Peter Büchner is interested in the impact of cultural traditions that
are transmitted across family generations, challenging the idea that
in modern societies learning and allocation to positions in the world
of work as a significant part of the former kinship dependencies
between succeeding generations has been generalised to the societal
level. He defines differing amounts of cultural resources (social
capital) as social class differences between families, and relates social
class to generation by studying the ways in which families transmit
their social capital between succeeding generations, that is from
grandparents to parents to children. Grandparents' and parents'
strategies of transmission aim at shaping the life trajectories of the
children in special ways; as the adults do this in competition with
other families, and as the children also act in competition with their
peers, this leads to distinctive family ways of culture transmission.

Peter Büchner is especially interested in how a trend towards
democratisation in personal contacts between parents and children,
and towards an individualisation of children's ways of shaping daily
life (which he and his colleagues investigated earlier) impacts on
recent changes in families' strategies for directing their children's life
courses. 'Family micro-cultures and processes of transgenerational
transmissions' can be studied in order to identify 'how family
resources are used for the shaping of lifecourses in different
generations ... Social and cultural capital are thus viewed as family
resources with a changing transmissibility' (Chapter 3, page 76). As
Peter Büchner argues, the family is still an important agency of
intergenerational transmission of culture and ways of life. The impact
of the family is not much reduced by shifts in the power balance
between parents and children, nor by the fact that many 'experiences
and skills (of the older generation) have become obsolete as the pace
of social change quickens' (Chapter 3, page 83).

Berry Mayall uses the UK social scene to explore interrelations
between the social status of women and of children, and argues that
in order to understand each, we need to take account of interactive

processes between both gender and generation. Children's lives are both influenced by and in turn influence women's lives. Their fortunes are closely linked through tradition, social policy, family structures and emotional ties. Berry Mayall argues that changes in the social condition and status of women will lead to changes in the social condition of children, and vice versa. For instance, mothers' entry into paid work means that children's daily life will change but, perhaps more importantly, children's relations to the state will change as it takes on more direct responsibility for standards of childcare. In turn, as children move out of the private sphere and take part in public institutions, the balance of responsibility for them shifts (somewhat) from mothers towards the state.

Generation and gender come into play in at least two ways in these processes. Relations between children and mothers are between people belonging to differing generation groups – born at differing points in time – and these child-adult relations are mediated through gender issues. But children and their mothers belong to differing 'actual' generations (in Mannheim's sense), since they have been exposed to differing sets of social pressures and events, and respond to these. Ideas about childhood and about motherhood may be thought to be undergoing change as the daily lives of children and their mothers change. In the UK these changes are slow to take place but, for instance, whilst mothering remains key to child health in public discourse it is no longer taken for granted that mothers should be at home full time with their young children. The generational order – how child-adult relations are understood at societal level – is slowly shifting.

Forming children's identity as a socio-cultural generation

The particular German interest in the concept of youth generations may be understood by taking account of the radical changes in the German society's political system, social structure and dominating ideas at the end of the first world war, at the beginning of the national-socialist regime, at the end of the second world war and in the late 1960s, when a generation which was not involved in the Hitler period became radical supporters of cultural democratisation (the 'anti-authoritarian movement'). In more recent times the societal transformation of East Germany after the end of the GDR has been another radical change. Does this mean that the adequacy of Mannheim's generation concept is dependent on such dramatic events? How are aspects of children's everyday life and of the position of childhood in society experienced by children of today, and how does that experience form their consciousness of identity as children? On the other hand, how are children's experiences in everyday life influenced by their feelings of belonging to a generation? The answers suggested in this book relate to children's agency and identity formation in everyday life.

Heinz Hengst focuses on the rising importance of the way children handle media and consumer goods. He is interested in 'the traces that socio-cultural change – such as media development and commercialisation – have left and are leaving behind in the collective orientations and patterns in children's conceptual world, in their notions of "us" and "them"' (Chapter 5, page 120). In this realm of daily life he questions the relations between the speed of social change and the emergence of differing cultural generations. He argues that in Mannheim's time, the 1920s, social change was taking place so fast that 'the non-contemporaneity of the contemporaneous' could be grasped by studying differences between succeeding generations. What about social change today? Today, the character of the intergenerational transfer of culture seems to change: the former knowledge-lead of the elder generation not only diminishes, it even becomes reversed when the young are the more competent, and this is the case in the realm of knowledge about media and consumption. Here, media have brought the age groups nearer together. Differentiations become more horizontal. The traditional two-generations model is influenced by new 'collective forces' created by the market. The market is scripting children as media users and consumers by creating '"imagined communities" of present-day children' (see Chapter 5, page 120) which are globalised and refer more and more to children of younger age groups. Such 'imagined communities' place children besides adults as a group with special needs and interests – a dehierarchisation – and this means a change in intergenerational relations. But how do children themselves integrate 'the market's scripts' in their 'identity work', that is, in their conceptualising of childhood? Heinz Hengst points to children's orientation to commercially produced culture and to how they differ from adults in the ways they emphasise the excitement, amusement and fun they get from media and consumer goods. He concludes that children's childhood concepts are more and more oriented to media and lifestyle, and in this they are, like adults, part of a 'western lifestyle' that overrides age groups and generational difference. But at the same time, the horizontal differentiation of lifestyles, although being a phenomenon of fragmentation, pluralisation and individualisation, is used by children to constitute childhood as 'fundamentally different' from adulthood.

Issues of cultural understanding are also important in Pia Christensen and Alan Prout's exploration of interconnections between space, place and generation. In the light of recent social theory, they define 'space' as a way of delineating a three-dimensional physical environment, in which objects and events occur in positions related to each other. But 'place' has an extra dimension; it is space invested with human meaning and significance. When people interact with the natural world, they invest it with culture; they make it their own and they make themselves part of it. Recent fieldwork (Christensen 2003) with children in the area (space) where they live and work shows that they understand these spaces as places, linked to their own experiences and social relations.

Pia Christensen and Alan Prout use fieldwork examples to demonstrate how three differing notions of generation are brought into play by children in their discussions of features of their locality. Firstly, a traditional anthropological interest is in the generational order: generation as a component of kinship systems. Children may refer to places as significant, for instance, because their grand-parents live/d there. Secondly, the Mannheimian concept, the authors argue, is essentially concerned with the passage of time and the emergence of groups who identify themselves and recognise others as having common experience as a generation group or cohort. But such common experiences may be understood as located not only in time, but also in space and place. Thirdly, in structural concepts of childhood, it is useful to study the way generational relations are produced or shaped by the wider generational order: socio-political influences. An example is the way in which UK education 'reforms' (National Curriculum, testing, competition between schools) have structured adult-child relations, so that teachers felt unable to find the time to harness children's own experiences, knowledge and understandings of place, but instead thought they should require children to absorb spatial ideas and knowledge independently of their bodily sensing and movement through a locality.

Historical dynamics in the development of childhood

Mannheim's interest in historically located generations was motivated by his interest in social change, in how it comes about and in its dynamics. This led him to focus on differences in ideas and social perceptions between succeeding generations, and on intergenerational conflicts resulting from such differences. Follow-ing Pinder, he questioned social dynamics that result from the 'contemporaneity of the non-contemporaneous' ('Gleichzeitigkeit des Ungleichzeitigen') (Mannheim 1952 [1928]: 283). Since each generation's thinking is based in another historical time, differing generations living together at a time are confronted with each other's particular way of thinking.

In Germany, studies of confrontations between historical gener-ations have been undertaken using biographical analyses. Recently, Gabriele Rosenthal (1997) has studied taboos and conflicts in transmission processes within families, with reference to the transmission of Second World War experiences of national-socialist activities and ideas between grandparents, parents and children. In the early 1980s a group of sociologists described the 'children-of-the-World-War-Two-generation' in terms of control relations and conflicts in everyday life situations (Preuss-Lausitz *et al.* 1983). As children they had had particular experiences of aspects of their parents' behaviour caused by war situations, and later, when they were young adults, these experiences influenced their way of challenging their parents' social and political concepts. When going on to study later-born 'childhood generations', the researchers emphasised what happens in childhood and how the positions in social structure and in power relations differ between children and adults. This description of historically specific intergenerational relations between children and adults became one of the starting points of childhood sociology in Germany.

Helga Zeiher's chapter discusses the approach of the 1983 study and goes on to present three successive West German 'childhood generations'. She aims to show how social changes in childhood and the generational order should be explained not only in terms of general trends and upheavals at the level of society at large and of social policy, but also in terms of individual experiences of events and changes which differ, as Mannheim noted, for succeeding generations. Particular experiences influence the ways in which members of a generation (in Mannheim's sense), as adults, construct and reconstruct childhood on the level of institutional structures and concepts. But differing historical backgrounds of adults' and children's ways of living and thinking also influence their personal interrelationships in everyday life. Their ways of interacting in everyday life construct childhood and generation relations on the societal level as well. Thus dynamics in personal generation relationships can produce dynamics in the development of societal childhood and vice versa. Helga Zeiher argues that each childhood generation is characterised by its own 'theme', be it fighting against control (the war children's theme) or searching for a balance between autonomy and social belonging (the theme of the children of the war children).

Results and suggestions for childhood sociology

Looking at the relations between the chapters of this book, we would argue for the usefulness of interconnecting both concepts of generation; that is, the concept of a childhood generation structure opposing or confronting an adulthood generation structure within a society's generational order, and the quite different concept of generation groups of people who are born at about the same time in history and are members of their generation for life.

How childhood is constructed in a society – for instance, by the organisation and conceptualisation of education, or by children's access to resources and rights – is embedded in the construction of the whole society; the generational order is formed by overwhelming economic, political and cultural structures, and it is intertwined with other societal orders such as gender (see Chapter 4) or social class structure (see Chapter 3). The condition of societal childhood at a time and in a region occurs within the concrete situations where individual children live their daily lives. When children interact with adults they experience these adults' generation-specific interpretations and uses of such situations and expectations towards their behaviour (see Chapter 3) – generation-specific in both senses. Children realise their agency and make their experiences in such concrete contexts, thereby forming their identity as children (see Chapter 6) which may – in particular historic contexts – later make them feel they are a historical generation group of their own (see Chapter 7). On the other hand, children influence and modify their concrete situations and their adult partners' ways of thinking and behaving by their agency, and by doing so they 'do generationing', that is constructing social childhood as a generational structure (see Chapter 1).

Thus 'generationing' happens in a dynamic field of – on the socio-structural level – the opposing generational structures of childhood and adulthood, and of – on the level of individual agency – more or less conflicting interactions between children and adults, each being members of differing generation groups. The two concepts of generation are related within the dynamics of social change. If we want to study social change in childhood, we should be aware of all processes in this dynamic field. And we should study not only 'outcomes' of such processes, such as features of particular generation groups of children or of particular childhood structures, but also study the changing of the processes (see Chapter 5). Today we have to be aware of changes that sociologists call blurring of boundaries between social structures in many realms of our society. Some of the boundaries between childhood and adulthood have become less strong, not least because media and markets offer access through the same routes to both children and adults, even if these access routes distinguish between the content of children's and adults' cultures. Today the questions asked by the sociology of childhood about the asymmetry of power relations and division of economic resources between childhood and adulthood, and between children and adults, are still very important. Yet the processes of children's identity formation as children and as a generation group (see Chapter 2) are of increasing interest, when culture is less frequently transmitted by adult persons and more often grasped by children themselves from anonymous information sources.

Notes

1 Karl Mannheim was born in 1893 in Hungary and emigrated in 1919 to Germany, where he became an influential sociologist. In 1933 he had to leave his professorship in Frankfurt and to emigrate again, this time to London. He taught at the London School of Economics and at the Institute of Education, where he was appointed to a chair in education, which he held for a year until his death in 1947 (Whitty 1997: 2–5).

2 For recent review see Zinnecker 2002.

References

Alanen, L. (2001) 'Childhood as a generational condition: Children's daily lives in a central Finland town'. In L. Alanen and B. Mayall (eds), *Conceptualising Child-Adult Relations*. London: RoutledgeFalmer.

Alanen, L. and Mayall, B. (eds) (2001) *Conceptualizing Child-Adult Relations*. London: RoutledgeFalmer.

Beck, U. (1992) *Risk Society*. London: Sage.

Bradley, B.S. (1989) *Visions of Infancy: A critical introduction to child psychology*. Cambridge: Polity Press.

Brannen, J. and Moss, P. (2002) 'An intergenerational study of employment and care'. *End-of-project report to Economic and Social Research Council*. Swindon: ESRC.

Büchner, P. (1990) 'Growing up in the eighties: changes in the social biography of childhood in the FRG'. In L. Chisholm, P. Büchner, H.-H. Krüger and P. Brown (eds), *Childhood, Youth and Social Change: A comparative perspective*. London: Falmer.

— (1995) 'The impact of social and cultural modernization on the everyday lives of children'. In M. du Bois-Reymond, R. Diekstra, K. Hurrelmann and E. Peters (eds), *Childhood and Youth in Germany and the Netherlands*. Berlin and New York: de Gruyter.

Christensen, P. (2003) 'Place, space and knowledge: children in the village and the city'. In P. Christensen and M. O'Brien (eds), *Children in the City: Home, neighbourhood and community*. London: RoutledgeFalmer.

Cunningham, H. (1991) *The Children of the Poor: Representations of childhood since the seventeenth century*. Oxford: Blackwell.

Ecarius, J. (ed) (1998) *Was will die jüngere mit der älteren Generation? Generationsbeziehungen und Generationenverhältnisse in der Erziehungswissenschaft*. Opladen: Leske und Budrich.

Edmunds, J. and Turner, B.S. (2002) *Generations, Culture and Society*. Buckingham: Open University Press.

Hendrick, H. (1994) *Child Welfare: England 1872–1989*. London: Routledge.

James, A. and Prout, A. (eds) (1997 [1990]) *Constructing and Reconstructing Childhood: Contemporary issues in the sociological study of childhood*. London: Falmer.

Jenks, C. (ed) (1982) *The Sociology of Childhood: Essential readings*. London: Batsford.

— (1996) *Childhood*. London: Routledge.

Kaufmann, F.-X. (1993) 'Generationenbeziehungen und Generationenverhältnisse im Wohlfahrtsstaat'. In K. Lüscher and F. Schultheis (eds),

Generationenbeziehungen in 'postmodernen' Gesellschaften. Konstanz: Universitätsverlag Konstanz.

Kessen, W. (ed) (1965) *The Child*. New York: John Wiley and Sons.

Kohli, M. (1985) 'Die Institutionalisierung des Lebenslaufs'. *Kölner Zeitschrift für Soziologie und Sozialpsychologie*, 37, 1–29.

Kohli, M. and Szydlik, M. (eds) (2000) *Generationen in Familie und Gesellschaft*. Opladen: Leske und Budrich.

Kränzl-Nagl, R., Mierendorff, J. and Olk, T. (2003) *Kindheit im Wohlfahrtsstaat: Gesellschaftliche und politische Herausforderungen*. Frankfurt am Main: Campus.

Liebau, E. and Wulf, C. (eds) (1996) *Generation: Versuche über eine pädagogisch-anthropologische Grundbedingung*. Weinheim: Deutscher Studien-Verlag.

Lüscher, K. and Schultheis, F. (eds) (1993) *Generationenbeziehungen in 'postmodernen' Gesellschaften*. Konstanz: Universitätsverlag Konstanz.

Mansel, J., Rosenthal, G. and Tölke, A. (eds) (1997) *Generationen-Beziehungen, Austausch und Tradierung*. Opladen: Westdeutscher Verlag.

Mannheim, K. (1952 [1928]) 'The problem of generations'. In K. Mannheim (ed), *Essays in the Sociology of Knowledge*. London: Routledge and Kegan Paul.

May, D. and Strong, P. (1980) 'Childhood as an estate'. In R.G. Mitchell (ed), *Child Health in the Community*. London: Churchill Livingstone.

Mayall, B. (2002) *Towards a Sociology for Childhood: Thinking from children's lives*. Buckingham: Open University Press.

Mayer, K.-U. and Müller, W. (eds) (1987) 'Lebensverläufe und Wohlfahrtsstaat'. In A. Weymann (ed), *Handlungsspielräume: Untersuchungen zur Individualisierung und Institutionalisierung von Lebensläufen in der Moderne*. Stuttgart: Enke.

Pilcher, J. (1994) 'Mannheim's sociology of generations: an undervalued legacy'. *British Journal of Sociology*, 45 (3), 481–495.

Pilcher, J. and Wagg, S. (eds) (1996) *Thatcher's Children: Politics, childhood and society in the 1980s and 1990s*. London: Falmer.

Pinder, W. (1926) *Das Problem der Generationen in der Kunstgeschichte Europas*. Berlin: Frankfurter Verlagsanstalt.

Preuss-Lausitz, U., Büchner, P., Fischer-Kowalski, M., Geulen, D., Karsten, M.E., Kulke, C., Rabe-Kleberg, U., Rolff, H.-G., Thunemeyer, B., Schütze, Y., Seidl, P., Zeiher, H. and Zimmermann P. (1983) *Kriegskinder, Konsumkinder, Krisenkinder: zur Sozialisationsgeschichte seit dem Zweiten Weltkrieg*. Weinheim and Basel: Beltz.

Prout, A. (2002) 'Researching children as social actors: an introduction to the Children 5–16 Programme'. *Children and Society*, 16 (2), 67–76.

Qvortrup, J. (1985) 'Placing children in the division of labour'. In P. Close and R. Collins (eds), *Family and Economy in Modern Society*. London: Macmillan.

— (1991) *Childhood as a Social Phenomenon: An introduction to a series of national reports*. Vienna: European Centre.

— (1994) 'Childhood matters: an introduction'. In J. Qvortrup, M. Bardy, G. Sgritta and H. Wintersberger (eds), *Childhood Matters: Social theory, practice and politics*. Aldershot: Avebury Press.

Rosenthal, G. (1997) 'Zur interaktionellen Konstitution von Generationen'. In J. Mansel, G. Rosenthal and A. Tölke (eds), *Generationen-Beziehungen, Austausch und Tradierung*. Opladen: Westdeutscher Verlag.

Schelsky, H. (1957) *Die skeptische Generation: Eine Soziologie der deutschen Jugend*. Düsseldorf: Diederichs.

Skolnick, A. (1975) 'The limits of childhood: conceptions of child development and social context'. *Law and Contemporary Problems*, 39 (3), 38–77.

Whitty, G. (1997) *Social Theory and Education Policy: The legacy of Karl Mannheim*. London: Institute of Education.

Zinnecker, J. (2002) 'Das Deutungsmuster Jugendgeneration: Fragen an Karl Mannheim'. In J. Zinnecker and H. Merkens (eds), *Jahrbuch Jugendforschung 2/2002*. Opladen: Leske and Budrich.

Part One
Processes of producing generation: theoretical frameworks

1 Childhoods: the generational ordering of social relations[1]

Leena Alanen

The project of constructing a sociology of childhood can be seen to have started in the 1980s. It first appeared in the form of a few isolated voices that drew critical attention to the ways in which children were (mis-)presented in the empirical and theoretical knowledge of social science: hardly at all, marginally at best, and, when so presented, they were seen merely 'as an afterthought' and support for the main construction or argument (Jenks 1982: 2 seq). In any case, they were not taken seriously and studied in their own right (Hardman, as early as 1973).

The project grew, has continued to grow, and has moved the scientific concern for children and childhood from its traditional primary location within the fields of developmental psychology, education and socialisation research to a broader area, giving it a legitimate place within social science. Childhood is now analysed as a part of society and culture, not just their precursor, and children are included in analysis as social actors, not just as beings who are in the process of becoming such (for example, James and Prout 1997: ix).

The social and scientific background to the emergence of the new field of childhood sociology is complex. Some of its bases, both external and internal to social science, have been identified. Just one significant external basis is the observation – a permanent public worry – that the social worlds in which today's children are living and growing up are rapidly and dramatically changing, both domestically and globally (for example, du Bois-Reymond *et al.* 1994). A further sign of the impact of broader societal transformations of childhood, variously identified under the title of 'modernisation', is that the familiar and customary social relations between childhood and adulthood, and between children and adults – or as I would argue, the *generational orders* of nation-states – are also being transformed. In accounting for the impact of modernisation on childhood and for the resulting novel forms of children's everyday life, one can no longer avoid including children in the analysis as subjects, actors and participants in the social (that is, material and cultural) world.

Significant among the bases internal to social science have been the postpositivist and emphatically 'constructionist' trends in the metatheories and methodologies of the day (see for example Prout and James 1997): they have strongly supported the emerging sociology of childhood and its deliberate concern with acting, feeling and knowing children, while also adding a 'deconstructive' strand to the study of childhood(s).

Summarising the developments in the field, three principal lines of work present in today's sociology on children and childhood can be identified.

The sociology of children (also identified as the ethnography of childhood) takes as its starting point the idea that children are worth studying in themselves 'in their own right' and from their own perspectives. Children are social actors in the social worlds they participate in, and research should focus directly on them and their living conditions, activities, relationships, knowledge and experiences. Internationally, this is the most widely followed line in childhood sociology.

A deconstructive sociology of childhood is grounded in post-positivist methodologies and their (constructionist) implications for social research (Foucault being the main inspiration). Here, any social notions of the child, children or childhood are treated as socially constructed discursive formations through which ideas, images and knowledge of children and childhood are communicated in social life. Often incorporated in broader social models of action and cultural practices, they also provide cultural scripts and rationales for people to act on children and also for children to act. This line of research implies that 'deconstruction' of such formations – cultural ideas, images, models and practices of children and childhood – is needed in order to disclose their (discursive) power in social life.

In a structural sociology of childhood, childhood is viewed as a (relatively) permanent element, and a part of the social structure of modern societies: it can be seen as a 'structure' in itself, comparable and analogous to, for instance, class and gender. Actual living children appear in this view assembled under the socially formed category of children, which Jens Qvortrup, a prominent advocate of this kind of sociology, calls 'childhood' (see for instance Qvortrup 1994). The goal of research is to link any relevant observed 'facts' at the level of children's lives (such as their social or economic condition, political status, or sense of identity) with their macro-level contexts, and to 'explain' the former by referring to the social structures and social mechanisms operating in this macro-context and generating the facts on the level of the child grouping.

Generationing the sociology of childhood

In the rest of this chapter, I will argue that even though the very basic tenet of any sociology of children/childhood is that the social phenomenon of childhood is above all a *generational* phenomenon, this insight has so far been barely touched upon in the 'new' social study of childhood, and even less worked into its conceptualisation – an odd situation indeed! Clearly, then, the sociology of childhood is itself in need of 'generationing'.

One promising route for bringing generation into the study of childhood is to take a new look at the work of Karl Mannheim (the foremost sociologist of 'generation') and to make use of the link upon which his theorising is actually built (though it was not fully developed by either him or his followers). Mannheim based his idea of (cultural) generations, their historical emergence and their role in social change on a particular understanding of social class. Based on this hint from Mannheim, it can be argued that the analogy between 'class' and 'generation' is theoretically more potent than Mannheim himself needed to realise for his own project, and that class (and gender) concepts in fact provide exciting possibilities for making 'generation' theoretically more useful for the study of childhood.

'Generation' is a term used conventionally in natural language and in everyday discourse, and several senses, or meanings, have been imported into social research. The notion and studies based on the term already have a place in social analysis; their significance and the work they could do for developing understandings of childhood is, however, fairly unexplored.

Particularly important here is the career of generation as a concept, and in recent years Mannheim's theorising has been (re)found to be valuable for developing sociological analysis in many areas. While many social scientists have picked up his legacy and continued to work within it (Pilcher 1994), this legacy has also generated pressure for more precise distinctions (for instance, regarding the differences between generation, age and cohort), expanding the area of generational analysis.

Mannheim's 'generation'

Mannheim is deservedly celebrated as the first scholar to bring 'generation' into sociology (Pilcher 1994; Eyerman and Turner 1998), in a long essay that he wrote at the end of the 1920s (Mannheim 1952 [1928]). He worked out his notion of generations within the frame of the sociology of culture (Matthes 1985; Corsten 1999: 53); generations were therefore to be understood and investigated as cultural phenomena, formed within specific social and historical contexts. Mannheim, moreover, argued that generations are formed when members of a particular age group (or cohort) live their youth through the same historical and social events and experience these events as significant to themselves. Through such shared experience they come to develop a common consciousness, which is observable even to outsiders and expressed in a shared world view and social and political attitudes. Moreover, these world views and attitudes tend to persist over the lifecourse of the cohort members, making membership in the same (cultural) generation easily identifiable to members themselves and to others even in later life.

Furthermore, Mannheim presented his theory of generations as a theory of social change or, as he expressed it, a theory of 'intellectual evolution' (Mannheim 1952 [1928]: 281): he thought that these culturally formed groups will and do act as collective agents and (cultural) bearers of social transformation (Becker 1997: 9–10, cf Mannheim, 1952 [1928]: 292–308). A generation, then, is a historically positioned age group whose members undergo a similar socialisation process, which brings about a shared frame of experience and action and makes them into an 'actual' generation. Mannheim therefore puts a clear emphasis on socialisation as the social 'mechanism' for generating cultural generations and, through them, also cultural change.

This reliance on socialisation as a central mechanism for bringing about generational phenomena is in interesting tension with some of the paradigmatic (Prout and James 1997) assumptions of the new sociological thinking of childhood. The idea of socialisation is after all one of the most critical points, or perhaps the most critical point in this rethinking of children and childhood. How then does, or would, Mannheimian thinking in terms of cultural generations fit into the various lines of recent childhood sociology?

'Generation' in sociologies of childhood

The notion of generation, it seems, has no particular part to play in organising the particular approach referred to above as the sociology of children. Although for the purpose of a study children may well be identified and named as a generational group, in distinction to other groups (such as babies, young people, adults, the elderly), this categorisation does not add anything to the conceptual framing of the approach. Studying children's relationships with and their experiences or views of other generational groupings also fits well into the basic paradigm of the sociology of children. Such issues, however, are in principle no more and no less topical and interesting to study than are, for instance, children's relationships with or experiences and views of disabled people, people belonging to various ethnic groups, or any other issue of social difference, or in fact any social issue. Therefore, 'generation' and the generational merely serve here as descriptive notions. They may well be brought into use but they nevertheless make a limited contribution to the main goal of research describing and understanding children's lives and their experiences of the social world.

In the deconstructive sociologies, 'generation' and the generational again merely serve as description, having no particular analytical role to play in organising the research approach. If they come into use at all, the way they are used and their inherent meanings would be as social objects to be deconstructed: contextualised, historicised and relativised.

In contrast to these first two sorts of childhood sociology, 'generation' becomes an explicit concern when the (historically varying) childhood phenomenon is brought into a structural frame. Now 'generation' indeed has a role to play, for it names the social (macro-)structure (the generational order) that is understood to distinguish children as a population group from other groups, and actually to 'constitute' them as a particular social category, through existing relations of social division, difference and inequality. This is a specific structural notion of generation, and I will later contrast it with other ways of thinking about structure. It is particularly useful in the promotion of comparative studies of the social conditions and circumstances in which the members of the social category of children live, in relation to those of adults or any other generational category, and allows us to draw politically significant conclusions, for instance on distributive justice among population groups and the relative position of children in such distributions (for instance of poverty; see Qvortrup 1994; Saporiti 1994; Sgritta 1994; Qvortrup 2000).

The conclusion from this short and limited review is that so far sociologists of childhood have not worked with 'generation' very much. That generations do exist and that children do form a generational group are most likely to be implied understandings based on everyday discourse rather than on grounded assumptions, with no clear recognition of their significance for theorising childhood.

In a way this appears as an odd conclusion, in the face of the clear and observable fact that the social worlds in which children live and act are generationally structured, and powerfully so. In our societies there exists the practically effective – and in this sense *real* and not just 'culturally constructed' – category of children; both our everyday experience and social research show that membership of this category – as well as of its counter-category of adults – makes huge differences in terms of the activities, opportunities, experiences, limitations, relationships and identities available for children across a number of institutions and domains of social activity.

Only the last strand of childhood sociology – the one operating with structures – points to this important but underdeveloped and under-theorised area. Understanding the specific generational structures in which children today live and in which their childhoods are generated, however, calls for more varied studies and more effective conceptual and methodological tools than are offered by the three kinds of childhood sociology presented above. Mannheim's seminal work on generations provides good grounds for developing such tools.

Mannheim's legacy and beyond

For decades after Mannheim's now famous essay on the 'problem of generations' was published, there was not much discussion of the subject in sociology. Later Mannheim's thinking did find some response, but mainly in a few small sub-disciplines, such as the study of youth groups and youth cultures.

Since the 1960s, however, scholars working in other areas of social research, such as social demography, lifecourse analysis and gerontology, have taken a new look at Mannheim's theory of generations and made use of it. Some of the confusions found in earlier uses of 'generation' have been resolved, and more precise and useful distinctions and conceptualisations have been developed. Specific research programmes have also evolved, such as 'generations research' or, more accurately, 'cohorts and generations research' (for instance, Becker 1997).

Today research on generations in the Mannheimian tradition has forged a niche for itself within social analysis. But can sociologists of childhood profit from this development? They might want, at least, to question its exclusive emphasis on the significance of experiences in youth for the emergence of generations. Children are the obvious fresh cohort entering social life, and should therefore be capable of sharing experiences in historical time and place, that is, of being a potential generation in Mannheim's sense. If we accept that children, too, are participants in social life (thereby rethinking Mannheim's socialisation thesis), then the Mannheimian frame should be fully applicable (possibly with modifications) in childhood research too.

However, outside this specific research niche generational issues have not been given much sociological attention. Interestingly, in the research literature about generational matters, age – and not generation – seems to be the emerging topic, especially in structurally tuned accounts of social divisions.[2] In Britain, for instance, Harriet Bradley, in a book subtitled *Changing patterns of inequality* (Bradley 1996), sees age as a more important 'dimension of stratification' than generation, devoting one full chapter to 'Age: the neglected dimension of stratification'. Janet Finch (1986: 12) writes that the use of age in ways that are theoretically informed and empirically rigorous is still 'relatively uncharted territory', while Jane Pilcher (1994: 482) strikes a balancing note by writing that 'the neglect of the sociology of generations parallels the lack of attention paid to the social significance of age'.

There is, however, still more to discover – or in fact rediscover – in 'generation', by going beyond the line of analysis that has followed from Mannheim's important work. In recent decades, gender, class, ethnicity, disability – all of them social conditions comparable to childhood – have been submitted to a critical, deconstructive gaze, by first interpreting them as social constructions and then reconceptualising and researching them from a number of theoretical (postpositivist) perspectives. Gender continues to be discussed and analysed, and variously theorised as a material, social and/or discursive structure, while (social) class, has of course, throughout the history of social analysis, provided a central concept for explaining social divisions and structural inequalities. Ethnic studies and disability studies are more recent fields of research which bring into focus and redefine both 'race'/ethnicity and disability as socially constructed phenomena, and seek to generate theoretical perspectives for research on the these particular conditions of inequality and exclusion and their consequences.

There are good reasons to believe that sociologists will learn more about childhood as a social and specifically generational (structural) condition of difference, division and inequality, by working on the notion of generation as an analogue to class, gender, ethnicity or disability. This suggests that 'generation' needs to be brought into childhood studies, and childhood needs to be brought into generational studies. However, in 'generationing' the sociology of childhood, the basic premise of the new childhood studies – children's agency – would need to be given central concern.

Generation as social structure

One useful bridge leading from Mannheim's notion of generation towards a more structural notion is found in his own mode of reasoning, for he uses class as an analogue to generation. His argument is based on the idea of a 'generational location' as the structural – and not merely metaphorical – equivalent of 'class location'. But it is worth noting that the sense of class that he refers to is of the Weberian kind: membership of class is defined by a common location in the social and historical process and, therefore, membership of an age group (Mannheim 1952 [1928]: 291; compare Corsten 1999: 253).

Weberian class is essentially defined by the situation of members of a class: 'the probability of their enjoying the benefits of material goods, gaining a position in life and "inner satisfactions" as a result of a relative control over goods and skills' (Weber 1968 [1922]: 302). A class then means all those people who share the same class situation, that is: the same set of life chances and of opportunities in property and employment markets (Crompton 1998: 57; Turner 1999: 225). An alternative definition (more common in Marxist-inspired studies) exists, in which class is defined by the economic *relations* of production between the members of different classes.

It is important to note that both of these understandings of class are relational, but there is a significant difference between the two kinds of relations between individuals and categories (classes) of individuals outlined above: they may be external relations (as existing, for instance, between Weberian classes) or internal relations (as existing between, for instance, Marxist-defined classes). This distinction will be elaborated on later in this chapter. However, there are even more insights to be gained for a generational analysis of childhood by exploring different ways of carrying out class analysis.

In explicating two models of explanatory analysis, Erik Olin Wright (1996: 123–125; 1997: 1–2), distinguishes between 'independent variable' and 'dependent variable' disciplines. Class analysis, as well as gender analysis (and, I shall argue, generational analysis) can be done, first, in an 'independent variable' analysis mode: the idea is to explore the relationships between class (or gender, or generation), which is treated as the 'independent variable', and other phenomena. Alternatively, class, gender or generation can be investigated as 'dependent variables', the idea here being to look for any social, material, biological, psychological or cultural factors that can be understood to generate the gender, class or generational phenomena in question.

The former, independent variable case does not mean that all phenomena can be explained primarily in terms of class, gender or generation; in many cases it will prove that it is not an important determinant at all. However, the analysis is based on the conviction that class/gender/generation in many cases is a pervasive structural cause and therefore worth exploring in terms of its ramifications for a variety of local phenomena.

It seems clear to me that Mannheim did not develop his form of generational analysis to fit into the 'independent variable' discipline. He did not mean generation to be conceived as a 'pervasive social cause that can have ramifications for many social phenomena'; rather, the Mannheimian historical, social generation is a dependent variable for which a number of conceivable causes can exist. In his own theorising of how generations may come to be formed, he pointed to a number of possible 'causes', the primary cause being a 'particular kind of identity of location' that members of a cohort share. Thus it is the task of historical and sociological research to discover, in each concrete case of generations (the 'dependent variable'), the particular socio-historical conditions (the 'independent variables') in which individuals become conscious of their common situation and make this consciousness the basis of their group solidarity (Mannheim 1952 [1928]: 290).

Mannheim's generation is not a structure in the same sense as class (as in class analysis) is, and as gender too – and, extending the argument, alternative definitions of generation – can be understood to be. Social structure is, of course, a central concept in sociology and there is a wide disagreement about what it can be made to refer to. For instance, Porpora (1998) identifies four different sociological conceptions of structure prominent in the field. Structure is seen as:

- a stable pattern of aggregate behaviour

- lawlike regularities

- collective rules and resources (compare Giddens 1979)

- a system of relationships among social positions.

It is this last one that we find in the kind of class analysis that Wright proposes, and so classes, patriarchies and, for instance, ethnic modes of exclusion are all usefully viewed as systems of relationships among social positions. Similarly structured (and structuring) units are found also on the micro level. The family is such a case: it too can be seen as a structured/structuring system of relationships, linking to each other the husband/father, the wife/mother and the children, all of which are social positions (Porpora 1998: 343).

The relational view of generational structures

Here – albeit without naming the particular structure constituted by relationships between the parent/child positions – Porpora presents acase of a generational structure on one particular institutional site. Like social structures in general, the familial generational structure is:

- a nexus of connections among (generational) positions

- a structure that causally affects the actions of the holders of those positions

- a structure that is also causally affected by their actions (ibid: 345).

Here we have a case of structural relations that are internal (or *necessary*; see Sayer 1992: 88–92) relations in that one position (such as that of a parent) cannot exist without the other position (the child). In addition, parenting – that is, action taken by an individual in a parental position – is dependent on the action 'performed' by the individual in the child's position, and a change in one position is tied to change in the other position. Internally related phenomena, then, are strongly interdependent although, as Sayer notes (ibid: 89–91), the relationship need not be, and often is not, symmetrical in both directions. The familial generational structure, for instance, is (usually) one of asymmetry.

As noted earlier, the Marxist concept of economic class also clearly hinges upon internal relations: capital necessarily presupposes wage labour, and outside this relationship, it is no longer capital. However, in non-Marxist analyses as well as in popular discourse, classes (or, more often, strata) are usually defined in terms of shared attributes, such as income, education and status. Accordingly the 'class structure' is constructed by researchers, who 'classify' individuals according to their correspondence to the chosen criteria of class. The relations between such classes (that is, relationships among holders of class positions) are seen to be external and contingent, because the class positions do not reciprocally define and imply each other, as in internal (necessary) relations.

In his study on gender, Connell (1987) argues that it is useful to theorise gender (or gender structure, called also 'patriarchy' in some discourses) in terms of internal relations. His terminology is somewhat different from the above, and based on an examination of current frameworks for theorising gender in which he critically looks at 'categorical' theories of gender proposed in sociology (Connell 1987: 54–61). In a categorical analysis, the existing gender categories – that is, the categories of 'men' and 'women' – are taken for granted, and empirical relationships between them are studied. This form of analysis follows – in Wright's terminology – the model of an independent variable discipline. The problematic point in theorising gender in this way is that, by setting a simple line of demarcation between gender positions, these analyses do not pay attention to the process of how the gender categories and relations between the categories are constituted in the first place, and are subsequently reproduced or, potentially, transformed. Therefore, categorical theories of gender are forced to treat both genders in terms of internally undifferentiated, homogeneous and general categories, thereby inviting criticism of false universalism and even of falling back on biological thinking.

A similar risk is evident in existing structural approaches to childhood that identify the social category of children on the basis, mostly, of chronological age (for instance, Qvortrup 1994; 2000). Children, like adults, become in effect a demographical age category or, in more precise demographical terms, one or more birth cohorts of individuals. Through a translation of the 'generational' into the social construction of 'age', the analysis in fact moves close together the generations and cohorts strand of (quantitative) generational analysis. Qvortrup (2000: 90–1) goes on to interpret the (contingent) relations between the generational categories of children versus adults in an economic frame, arguing in terms of (macro-)economic processes which he uses to 'explain' the economic consequences of the age-related generational structuring for the childhood category. His mode of analysis can be viewed as a modification of Mannheim's generational analysis: children form a (potential) economic (and not cultural, at least not in the first place) generation in that they share the same set of economic risks and opportunities. The Mannheimian perspective suggests furthermore that the age group of children (through socialisation) may also develop shared cultural and attitudinal features, and additionally become a cultural generational group.[3]

What then does a relational conceptualisation of childhood imply? As we have seen, a relational analysis of childhoods can be carried out in terms of both external and internal relations. When children are defined externally, the basis for defining category membership is some observable similarity or shared attribute, or sets of them, among individual children. In practice, age turns out to the most commonly used attribute. But whichever defining property is chosen to make the categorisation, the relations among members of the child category – as also those between members of the two categories of children and non-children – remain external and contingent. The structural sociologies of childhood that have been proposed so far mainly follow this categorical approach (for instance Qvortrup 2000).

A different and theoretically novel conceptualisation of generational structures becomes possible by choosing to focus on the internal connections in children's relations to the social world. In this case the notion of a generational structure (or generational order – compare Connell's 'gender order') refers to the complex set of social (relational) processes through which some people become (or are 'constructed' as) 'children' while other people become (are 'constructed' as) 'adults' (see, for example, Alanen 1992; Honig 1999; Alanen 2001b). 'Construction' necessarily involves agency, in this case of both children and adults, and it is most usefully understood as a practical and even material process, and studied as a social, generationing practice (compare Connell 1987), or perhaps a set of practices.[4] The conclusion, then, is that the two generational categories of children and adults are recurrently produced through such practices; because of the ongoing generationing practices they then stand in relations of connection and interaction, and of interdependence. Neither category can exist without the other, and what each of them is (a child, an adult) is dependent on its relation to the other. Change in one is necessarily tied to change in the other.

Childhoods: children's generationally structured relations

As emphasised at the beginning of the paper, a specific concern in exploring the generational structures within which childhood as a social position is daily produced as individually experienced childhoods is that children's agency is securely built into both the theory and the method. This is better guaranteed in relational thinking based on internal relations than in the structural approach that operates with the preconceived categories of age groups, which leaves unexplored the ways in which and by whom the structure is reproduced.

Moreover, the internal relations approach also allows that agency is not restricted to the micro-constructionist understanding of being a social actor, as tends to be the case in the sociology of children. Rather, agency is inherently linked to the 'powers' (or lack of them) of those positioned as children to influence, organise, coordinate and control events taking place in their everyday worlds. Such positional 'powers' are best approached by the researcher as possibilities and limitations of action, 'determined' by the specific structures (generational structures, regimes or orders) within which people are positioned as children. Therefore, in order to detect the range and nature of the agency of living children, the *generational structures* from which children's powers (or lack of them) derive need to be identified. The socially determined source of individuals' agency in their capacity as children is therefore to be found by investigating the particular social organisation of generational relations existing in the society under study. This, finally, provides the background to the fundamental importance of 'generation' for the development of sociological understandings of childhood.

Notes

1 This paper is based on Alanen (2001a; 2001b).
2 There is, moreover, an interesting difference (in need of explanation) between the British emphasis on the notion of age and the renaissance (Corsten 1999) of generational thinking in Germany.
3 Connell's route out of the analytical impasse he sees in categorical analysis is to move away from preconceived gender categories towards a 'practice-based' approach. This involves focusing not on external relations but on internal relations, in the sense of concentrating on the constitution of gender categories and also, therefore, on the constitution of gender structures. A focus on internal relations necessarily implies the study of process: in his case, of 'how gender relations are organised as a going concern' (1987: 63). Therefore, conceptualising gender in terms of internal relations has implications also for the methodology to be applied in empirical gender studies: it too has to be made consistently relational.
4 General accounts of relational methodologies in social science are given by, for instance, Bhaskar (1979); Bourdieu (1990: 123–39; 1998: 1–13); Bourdieu

and Wacquant (1992: 94–8); Swartz (1997: Chapter 6); Manicas (1998) and Scott (1998). Pierre Bourdieu argues strongly for a relationist methodology and contrasts it with a mode of thought that he (following Cssirer) calls 'substantialism', which 'leads people to recognise no realities except those that are available to direct intuition in ordinary experience, individuals and groups'. Relationalism (or relationism – Scott 1998) identifies the real not with substances but with relations, and sociology, according to this view, is the analysis of these relations, that is: 'relative positions and relations between positions' (Bourdieu 1990: 126; 1998: 3). 'The real is relational' (Bourdieu and Wacquant 1992: 232).

References

Alanen, L. (1992) *Modern Childhood? Exploring the 'child question' in sociology.* Publication Series A, 50. Jyväskylä: Institute for Educational Research, University of Jyväskylä.

— (2001a) 'Explorations in generational analysis'. In L. Alanen and B. Mayall (eds), *Conceptualizing Child-Adult Relations.* London: RoutledgeFalmer.

— (2001b) 'Childhood as a generational condition: children's daily lives in a central Finland town'. In L. Alanen and B. Mayall (eds), *Conceptualizing Child-Adult Relations.* London: RoutledgeFalmer.

Becker, R. (1997) 'Generationen und sozialer Wandel – eine Einleitung'. In R. Becker (ed), *Generationen und sozialer Wandel.* Opladen: Leske and Budrich.

Bhaskar, R. (1979) *The Possibility of Naturalism.* Hemel Hempstead: Harvester Wheatsheaf.

du Bois-Reymond, M., Büchner, P., Krüger, H.-H., Ecarius, J. and Fuhs, B. (1994) *Kinderleben. Modernisierung der Kindheit im interkulturellen Verglaich.* Opladen: Leske and Budrich.

Bourdieu, P. (1990) *In Other Words.* Cambridge: Polity Press.

— (1998) *Practical Reason.* Stanford: Stanford University Press.

Bourdieu, P. and Wacquant, L.J.D. (1992) *An Invitation to Reflexive Sociology.* Cambridge: Polity Press.

Bradley, H. (1996) *Fractured Identities: Changing patterns of inequality.* Cambridge: Polity Press.

Connell, R.W. (1987) *Gender and Power.* Cambridge: Polity Press.

Corsten, M. (1999) 'The time of generations'. *Time and Society,* 8, 2, 249–72.

Crompton, R. (1998) *Class and Stratification.* Cambridge: Polity Press.

Eyerman, R. and Turner, B.S. (1998) 'Outline of a theory of generations'. *European Journal of Social Theory,* 1 (1), 91–106.

Finch, J. (1986) 'Age'. In R. Burgess (ed), *Key Variables in Social Investigation*. London: Routledge and Kegan Paul.

Giddens, A. (1979) *Central Problems in Social Theory. Action, theory and contradictions in social analysis*. Berkeley, CA: University of California Press.

Hardman, C. (1973) 'Can there be an anthropology of children?'. *Journal of the Anthropological Society of Oxford*, 4 (1), 85–99.

Honig, M.-S. (1999) *Entwurf einer Theorie der Kindheit*. Frankfurt am Main: Suhrkamp.

James, A. and Prout, A. (1997) 'Preface to second edition'. In A. James and A. Prout (eds), *Constructing and Reconstructing Childhood*. London: Falmer Press.

Jenks, C. (1982) 'Introduction'. In C. Jenks (ed), *The Sociology of Childhood: Essential readings*. London: Batsford.

Manicas, P. (1998) 'A realist social science'. In M. Archer, R. Bhaskar, A. Collier, T. Lawson and A. Norrie (eds), *Critical Realism: Essential readings*. London: Routledge.

Mannheim, K. (1952 [1928]) 'The problem of generations'. In K. Mannheim (ed), *Essays in the Sociology of Knowledge*. London: Routledge and Kegan Paul.

Matthes, J. (1985) 'Karl Mannheims "Das Problem der Generationen", neu gelesen: Generationen-"Gruppen" oder gesellschaftliche Regelung von Zeitlichkeit?' *Zeitschrift für Soziologie*, 14 (5), 363–72.

Pilcher, J. (1994) *Age and Generation in Modern Britain*. Oxford: Oxford University Press.

Porpora, D.V. (1998) 'Four concepts of social structure'. In M. Archer, R. Bhaskar, A. Collier, T. Lawson and A. Norrie (eds), *Critical Realism: Essential readings*. London: Routledge.

Prout, A. and James, A. (1997) 'A new paradigm for the sociology of childhood? Provenance, promise and problems'. In A. James and A. Prout (eds), *Constructing and Reconstructing Childhood*. Second edition. London: Falmer Press.

Qvortrup, J. (1994) 'Introduction'. In J. Qvortrup, M. Bardy, G. Sgritta and H. Wintersberger (eds), *Childhood Matters: Social theory, practice and politics*. Aldershot: Avebury.

— (2000) 'Macro-analysis of childhood'. In P. Christensen and A. James (eds), *Research with Children: Perspectives and practices*. Aldershot: Avebury.

Saporiti, A. (1994) 'A methodology to make children count'. In J. Qvortrup, M. Bardy, G. Sgritta and H. Wintersberger (eds), *Childhood Matters: Social theory, practice and politics*. Aldershot: Avebury.

Sayer, A. (1992) *Method in Social Science*. London: Routledge.

Scott, J. (1998) 'Relationism, cubism, and reality: beyond relativism'. In T. May and M. Williams (eds), *Knowing the Social Worlds*. Buckingham: Open University Press.

Sgritta, G. (1994) 'The generational division of welfare'. In J. Qvortrup, M. Bardy, G. Sgritta and H. Wintersberger (eds), *Childhood Matters: Social theory, practice and politics*. Aldershot: Avebury.

Swartz, D. (1997) *Culture and Power: The sociology of Pierre Bourdieu*. Chicago: The University of Chicago Press.

Turner, B.S. (1999) *Classical Sociology*. London: Sage.

Weber, M. (1968 [1922]) *Economy and Society*. Berkeley, CA: University of California Press.

Wright, E.O. (1996) 'Marxism after Communism'. In S.T. Turner (ed), *Social Theory and Sociology: The classics and beyond*. Cambridge and Oxford: Blackwell.

Wright, E.O. (1997) *Class Counts*. Cambridge: Cambridge University Press.

2 Biographical revisions and the coherence of a generation

Michael Corsten

Wenn man zusammen jung gewesen ist,
dann ist, wenn man in Gnade ist,
die Sonne besonders schön.
Aber wenn man in Ungnade ist,
sind auch die Prügel besonders hart.
Jürgen W. Kuczynski, 1997

Quit recycling the past.
Douglas Coupland, 1991

The collective identity of generations? Why should we use such a concept?

To talk about collective identity is problematic for many reasons (Niethammer 2000). Let me briefly discuss two. First, one might ask if it makes sense at all to talk about collective identity. It can be argued that, from an analytical standpoint, such social phenomena have to be characterised by referring to individual actions; from a moral point of view, the attribution of collective qualities too easily becomes ideological. Second, dominant cultural patterns of contemporary societies tend to individualise symbolic meanings. What something means for me matters for me as a whole person, not as, for instance, a German, a Catholic, a white person or a man of 40. Although the terrorist destruction of the World Trade Centre and the Pentagon were massive attacks against representative buildings of the United States, these attacks were regarded, at least in the United

States, as a symbolic action, as an aggression against 'civilised societies'. It was not interpreted as an ethnic, religious or nationalist plot. And the military operations that followed were not described by the United States as a war against the Afghan people, but as a war against a regime that supported terrorists.

Contemporary globalisation processes include two cultural generalisations (Corsten 1999a): the inclusion of the world population within civilisation, and the individualisation of the single person regardless of his or her social, national, religious or ethnic origin. Given these two generalisations, a global civilisation would mean the end of distinctive collective identities. We would all be included in the global civilisation of mankind. And although social inequalities might remain, the discourse of globalisation would have deconstructed any attempts to legitimise inequalities based on collective identities.

Therefore the topic of generation raises the question of whether overall inclusion is the whole story. If the discourse of globalisation leads to a disclaimer of strong distinctive collective identity (as providing good reasons for social distinctions), does it, at the least, corrode all forms of collective ties?

Mannheim's concept of generation

To Karl Mannheim's credit is the discovery of the coherence of a generation as a weak tie of collective identity that is different in kind from national, religious or ethnic attributes. His famous paper 'The problem of generations' (1952 [1928]) was first published in the 1920s. He was confronted with rapid modernisation processes in the democracies established late on (compared to processes in other countries) after the First World War, especially in Hungary, Austria, Germany and Italy. Mannheim attempted to overcome the binary distinctions of 'community' and 'society' as guiding patterns for sociological analysis.[1] For him generation 'as actuality' was an example of a different form of social association. He distinguished explicitly between generations and other forms of social association, such as communities or membership of organisations. Starting with an analogy to social class, he elaborated a dialectic concept of collective identity, differentiating between generation as social location (as such), as actuality (for itself) and as unit (as such and for itself). Mannheim's use of the generation concept is integrative: for him generation is the coordination and integration of all three aspects – location, actuality, and unit.

Because this integrative view is rather complex and difficult, I will try to explain more about the different meanings of generation that are involved.

Generation as social location

This first dimension refers to the strata of experience as an opportunity structure of a generational location (site) – only people born and growing up at the same time have the opportunity to experience certain events and their succession simultaneously. Generation as location is equivalent to the more technical concept of birth cohorts (Ryder 1965).

The German term, 'Generationslagerung', differs slightly from the term 'Lage' which means 'location'. 'Lagerung' would be translated as 'storage'. Using this metaphor, one could say that Mannheim wanted to stress the sequential time order of historical experiences stored in the biographical memories of persons who belong to the same generation (birth cohort).

Generation as 'actuality'

The second dimension refers to the collective self-interpretation of people who belong to one generation. Mannheim calls it 'Generationszusammenhang' – a certain coherence between people belonging to the same generation. It does not mean the 'only real' or 'actual' expression of a generation, which English readers might mistakenly think when reading Mannheim's text in English.[2] Basically it focuses on a frame of interpretation shared by the members of a generation. This frame of interpretation is mainly a shared horizon of biographical and historical time. It is presupposed that people of one generation develop a common view of the 'historical new' during their biographical period of adolescence. Mannheim's original German is: 'Dieselbe Jugend, die an der selben historisch-aktuellen Problematik orientiert ist, lebt im gleichen Generationszusammenhang'; I would translate this as 'The same youth that is oriented towards the same historically-current complex of problems *lives in the coherence of a generation*'. The concept 'generation as "actuality"' should denote a form of social association – feeling related to each other by sharing a horizon of time perspectives, a dramatic coherence of past, presence, and future.

Generation as 'unit'

Third, Mannheim identifies concrete groups of people of the same age, who not only define their situation (time horizon) in a similar way but also develop similar ways of reacting in response to their generational problems and opportunities, as 'generational units'.

Generations, or more precisely people born at the same time in a given society, have common experiences of their social background and, in effect, feel related to each other because they share these experiences. This does not mean that members of one generation would all think and react in the same way as each other. Rather, they have a weak emotional tie which relates to their similar interpretation of their own biographical development and of the historical development of their society. For Mannheim (following Pinder 1926), the similarity resists in a shared horizon of time perspectives which are polyphonically organised. Mannheim is fully aware of the manifold social differences between and within generations, but considers that members of the same generation share a common sense – 'we-strata' (Bude 1997) – of the dominant constellations and principles by which their time was 'polyphonically organised'.

In particular, Mannheim's argument is that the same historical events, although relevant to the whole population living at the same time, are regarded differently by different generations. He proposes that the reason for this is that members of different generations experience the same historical event at a different 'stage' (or phase) of their life. For example, for one generation the beginning of a war takes place in their childhood, and for them war will be followed by peace in their youth; for an earlier generation the same war starts towards the end of their youth; for them, peace in their childhood was followed by war. Thus generations differ in their biographical ordering of the same historical events, and their interpretation of these events therefore originates from differing perspectives on events in historical time.

Beyond Mannheim (the transformations of Mannheim's legacy)

The debates and approaches following Mannheim's work tend to focus on particular aspects of his solution to the problem of generation (Pilcher 1994). I will mention seven important streams of investigation.

The cohort approach

This approach was formulated with reference to the idea of generational location (Ryder 1965; Glenn 1977; Kertzer 1983, O'Brien *et al.* 1989). The fact of being born at the same time – that is, of belonging by birth to a specific range of years – was taken to distinguish so-called 'birth cohorts'. In this type of research, the main problem deals with characteristics that members of birth cohorts do or do not share. The question is: do we observe cohort effects or not?

Sociological and psychological investigations

For the cohort approach it is not necessary to study concrete experiences of 'cohort members'. Such studies have mostly been investigations which combine sociological and psychological issues. The development of experiences and their effects on attitudes during the lifecourse is reconstructed via longitudinal studies. The classic example is Glen H. Elder's *Children of the Great Depression* (1974). Important investigators followed this line of research (Alwin 1991; Pronovost 1992; Mach 1994) but there are also similar approaches that are concerned with the question of collective memory of generations (Braungart and Braungart 1986; Schuman and Scott 1987; Lang *et al.* 1993; Jennings 1996; Schuman *et al.* 1997) and its development during the lifecourse.

Biographical research

In the first two approaches the problem of whether experiences of time exist in a more holistic or dramatic sense is left open (White 1986). These experiences are mostly studied in biographical research (Schelsky 1963; Bude 1987; Bertaux and Thompson 1993; Bertaux 1995; Bude 1995). The main sources of investigation in this third approach are narrations or life stories, which attempt to reconstruct dramatic patterns of biographical representation shared by the members of a generation. The leading question is: do members of the same generation use similar schemes, or so-called 'scripts' (Buchmann 1989) to describe their experiences of life?

The study of trends in youth and adolescence

This approach focuses on the description of themes and attitudes articulated by young people born at differing historical periods (Ferchhoff 1985; Jaide 1985; Attias-Donfut 1996; Grauers 1996; Ferchhoff 1997; Austin and Willard 1998). The observation of generations is restricted to age-specific (youth-only) attitudes and practices. This line of investigation is sometimes criticised as being too schematic and taking an over-simplified view of the succession of youth generations (Wensierski 1994). However, this stream of investigation led to the sociological and developmental psychological analysis of the life phase of adolescence. Whereas the sociological perspective is more interested in the 'transition into adulthood' (Marini 1984; Modell 1992; Huinink and Konietzka

2000), developmental psychology focuses on adolescence as a moratorium for identity (Döbert and Nunner-Winkler 1973; Erikson 1980; Marcia 1980; Stiksrud 1994; Habermas and Bluck 2000).

The analysis of specific groups

Another treatment of youth is through the analysis of specific groups, sometimes described as milieus or small cultures (Clarke 1976; Clarke *et al.* 1976; Hall and Jefferson 1976; Willis 1978; Bohnsack 1989; Maase 1995; Thornton 1995; Bohnsack 1997; Skelton and Valentine 1998). This type of investigation follows Mannheim's notion of a generational unit, regarded as a group of young people who experience being bound together because they have acted with common aims or in adherence to common principles.

Research on relations between differing generations

This research is also important and relevant (Eisenstadt 1956), particularly nowadays in the context of families. Here the so-called three-generational approach[3] (Rintala 1962) has been brought into play again in recent years (Völter 1996; Rauschenbach 1998; Hildenbrand 2000; see also Chapter 3). Using a cohort perspective, Lauterbach (1995) dealt with the co-residence of three generations in contemporary family life.

Discourse about generations

A final question that has been raised in recent years deals with the emergence and consequences of the discourse about generations (Attias-Donfut 1992; Brosziewski 2001). Here one asks not whether there really are generations or particular generational experiences but whether it is important to identify and communicate generational differences rather than other differences of gender or class. Achim Brosziewski (2001) pointed out (following Luhmann 1980) that the question of whether to talk about generations could be viewed as society's attempt to observe and thereby to structure social time.

In what sense can a generation establish a collective notion of itself? Four complexes of assumptions

These differing types of research have uncovered many inconsistencies and contradictions between the various concepts, and have been used to reject the integrative intention of Mannheim's original approach. In this section, I will discuss four basic complexes of assumptions that are required for an integrative concept of generation. The complexes of assumptions provide steps towards an answer to the above question.

The standardised structure of lifecourse development
The first set of assumptions is related to the idea that the dominant challenge for personal identity arises during so-called 'adolescence'. This complex of assumptions is guided by two perspectives.

The first perspective views adolescence as the period between youth and adulthood. Technically we can demarcate this period by the occurrence of particular events (Marini 1984). The end of youth can be defined by leaving high school (reaching the standard level of school education); the birth of one's first child and creating a family of one's own symbolises becoming an adult. The period between these two events is characterised by search processes (finding a job, a partner for life). The postulated life phase 'adolescence' depends importantly on the idea of the standardisation of the lifecourse as an ordered sequence of events, transitions and phases.

On the one hand, this idea should not be taken too strictly. It does not mean that each member of a generation experiences important transition events in their life at exactly the same time. On the other hand, the idea of an objective timetable that structures individual development in modernity has to be taken seriously within these assumptions. But this is more of a sociological idea than one postulated by developmental psychology. It says that the sequence of life events is ordered in a certain way, and that this order is established by collective belief in the appropriateness of moving through life, especially through transitory phases, in a particular way. Modern biographical scripts tell us what has to come first. That means that statistical observations of an age-standardisation of some important transitions in life (like the age of entering paid work, of first marriage, of having a first child) are affected by the rationalisation of the life concept (Meyer, 1986).

Martin Kohli (1985) has argued that the expectation of getting old (70 years or more), which has become secure in modern societies, enables individuals to plan things in their life. So it becomes rational to defer gratifications for attaining goals in later life. If I can be sure of experiencing a later life, I can start to ask what should precede particular goals. 'Take it as it comes' is no longer a valid rule for life; but ideas like 'first work and then play' are more appropriate. The success of the life concepts of developmental psychology (that is, success in terms of being believed) can then be explained by the possibility of a code of life based on a rationalised discipline; at least in Foucault's (1976) sense that the regulation modes of modern societies are based on controlling things and people by continuous reinforcement and reproduction.

Therefore – and this leads to the second perspective – within this framework of assumptions, the phase 'adolescence' is seen as an important precondition of becoming an autonomous and self-conducted person. That this phase in life is (often) age-standardised is not of critical importance. The reference to a certain age just provides a hint that people of that age have the important task of 'getting into one's own', as Modell (1992) expresses it. But 'getting into one's own' is an effect of the guiding script of life, of becoming a sovereign, autonomous, self-conducted person. Seen from this standpoint, events like 'leaving school', 'entering first job', 'having one's first child' imply social meanings concerning the grade of 'self-responsibility' of a person. Someone who has fulfilled the standard time of education in a (modern) society can be interpreted as a person who possesses the basic competences to conduct his or her own life. Therefore, the ending of the normal school time is a starting signal to 'get into one's own'. People are expected to decide self-responsibly how to get a job or whom they want to date and mate with. The birth of the first child, from this perspective, symbolises the highest grade of self-responsibility in modern societies. To take responsibility for the development of somebody else, for one's children, implies that someone is well prepared to act self-responsibly. This consideration is part of the theory that the standardisation of the lifecourse primarily lies in the rationalisation of life decisions. This is why, in the normative structure of the transitions to adulthood, education and occupational qualification should be concluded, and the entry into a stable occupation should have been realised before someone creates a family and has children. In this view adolescence is a time of preparation or, from the anthropologist's perspective, a time of initiation (Turner 1977).

The above theory is based upon a rational script of life. But this 'script' should not be interpreted as a merely discursive or symbolic artefact. It is relevant because of its practical consequences for one's 'conduct of life' ('Lebensführung'). The rules of this life phase cause a feeling of insecurity and indefiniteness concerning one's own self-definition. The age-standardisation means that people of one generation experience these feelings at the same historical and biographical time – and that means, at the least, together. 'Generation as actuality', therefore, refers to the background of this experience of biographical indefiniteness, including the task of overcoming it at a particular historical phase. And this is also the reason why a generation is so sensitive to, or likely to be influenced by, the historical time that their members have experienced as 'new' during their 'adolescence'.

I should like to add one important point: it is not only the historical periods of deep change or crisis that matter for generational experience. From the point of view of this theoretical assumption, it is to be expected that a generation will be influenced in their 'adolescence' by historical changes which another generation would not interpret as change. It depends on the members of a generation to discover the 'historical new' in the life phase of adolescence which they face simultaneously. This difference is precisely what makes for generational differences.

Collective identity

In what sense does this experience of the life phase of adolescence, which is historically parallel for the members of one generation, lead to 'collective identity'? And, in what sense can we talk sensibly about collective identity?

There are two difficulties inherent in the concept of identity. The first is the danger of relying on a rigid notion of identity as stable self-consistency. The second is the risk of reifying the aspect of 'collectivity'. So I start here with a more general definition of identity as reflexive self-reference. If individual or collective producers or creators of actions attribute the meaning of the action as being characteristic of themselves, this can be called self-reference, or at least 'identity' (White 1992; Straub 1998). If such self-referent attributions are compared with each other – that is, if actors recognise that two or more self-characterisations are consistent or inconsistent with each other – they refer to their collective identity. Collective identity, then, comprises both differences and similarities. Creators of actions might attribute to themselves differing (and even inconsistent) qualities, and they might notice that these self-attributions could have taken a differing form in a different situation.

How can someone – or a group – define herself, himself or themselves, despite being confronted by a diversity in their own experiences, actions, motifs and self-expressions? Identity – if personal or collective – is, in the first place, self-assertion ('Selbstbehauptung'). It involves struggling for significant definitions of one's self faced with the manifold definitions that could be attributed to a person or a collective. Thus identity is less a state than a process, the process of the contingent turns of or attempts at self-identification.

The collective self-identification of a generation takes place implicitly and *en passant* during processes of symbolic interactions. Therein members of a generation discover that they share a particular time horizon – a dramatic placement of historical events into their own biographical development. It is a vague presentiment for a particular framework of contemporary history. It is not assumed that this implicit form of collective self-discovery could be made explicit, or even reflexive. This depends on the next point, the intra-generational discourse of a generation, which can divide up into different generational units.

Intra-generational discourses

Although I wish to emphasise similarities in a generation, I should also point to important intra-generational differentiations. People of the same age who have been exposed to similar historical backgrounds in their 'adolescence' can respond to these with systematically distinctive and differing experiences, caused by social inequalities such as gender (Macpherson and Fine 1995; Chapter 1; Chapter 4), education, social origin (Mayer 1993; 2000; Chapter 3), ethnicity (Esser 1989; Siefen *et al.* 1996; Strom *et al.* 1996).[4] In Germany, the question of whether sub-cultural or youth-cultural differences may also be distinctions that generate intra-generational differentiations (Fischer-Kowalski 1983) has been debated since at least the 1980s.

Usually such intra-generational differentiations are seen as disabling the formation of a generation as an actuality. But no one has tried to turn the issue around: to regard intra-generational differentiations as discursive processes which are intrinsically a part of the formation of a collective generational background. From my point of view, this last hypothesis is in line with the adolescence thesis. If generations are sensitive to the collectively experienced time of adolescence they are also sensitive to the distinctions or 'battles of social distinctions' (Thornton 1995) that they are experiencing and perhaps fighting out during this life phase. That

means they have a certain practical knowledge held in common
regarding the symbolic battles of their youth. They are familiar with
the standpoints of those of their generation who stand in opposition
to them. They know about the weight (Falardeau 1987) that certain
symbolic moves have in this discursive practice. They have a nose
for the proportion of young people of their generation who would
follow a particular style. Knowing the rules of the game of symbolic
differentiation in one generation is at the least part of the discursive
and historical background that the members of one generation
share collectively.

Is there a collective imagery of childhood shared by members of a generation?

One question – in our context, the most important one – has been left
open. Why should the constitution of a generation happen in
adolescence? Or, to rephrase, why does it not take place in (earlier)
childhood?

Studies – especially concerning the so-called 1968 generation
(Preuss-Lausitz *et al.* 1983; Faimberg 1988; Bude 1995) – have
emphasised the importance of childhood for the constitution of a
generation.[5] Peter Büchner (Chapter 3) remarks that the depth of a
generation's historical experience would be the decisive point. The
massive and traumatic experiences that European children born
around 1940 had during World War Two could be an explanation for
a strong imagery of destruction which is visible in their autobio-
graphical speech (Preuss-Lausitz *et al.* 1983; Bude 1995).

Taking this example, one might ask what the strong and lasting
pictures for contemporary children will be. Are their images the
products of media cultures (Chapter 5)? The imagery of the children's
world could be an interesting starting point for the analysis of the
collective memory of a generation. Are their first pictures (destroyed
cities as 'free chosen playgrounds' in the late forties and fifties,
artificial playgrounds created by community architects in the late
sixties and seventies, the TV heroes Lassie, Flipper, and Fury in the

seventies and eighties, or the game boy figures of Pokemon and Digimon in the nineties) a kind of a dream world that remains in collective memory? One then has to ask: why do these pictures remain? What kind of power drives their retention?

However these questions are resolved, I would reiterate the relevance of biographical revisions. Some images may remain in collective memory. They might be a weight or a load for a generation which is guided by their first pictures. But biographical revisions will also take place in the collective lifecourse of birth cohorts. The collective entry into new life phases means that a generation is confronted with new challenges, biographically and historically. Generations do also learn in the sense that they can reject – or, less dramatically speaking, revise – their earlier attitudes. If, then, we regard generation as the process in which a collective horizon of an own time is revised, we will discover sequences of frameworks of historical and biographical memories. For instance, for the 1968 generation, childhood in the destroyed cities after World War Two was followed by adolescence in the cold war period, accompanied by a petit bourgeois middle-class climate (making this generation 'rebels without a cause'). This was followed by adulthood in a period of prosperity, leading this generation into early careers – especially in the system of public economy ('Marsch durch die Institutionen') – which in turn was followed by preparation for retirement in a long era of stagnation (from the mid-eighties), accompanied by questioning of the following generation's political commitment.[6] Helga Zeiher (Chapter 7) demonstrates her awareness of the importance of biographical revisions when she writes: 'The experience of liberty in early childhood and restriction in later childhood and adolescence, the clash between absence of control and its subsequent restoration made the war children born after 1939 a "generation as actuality"' (page 164). The question for the empirical study of generations is: how is a dramaturgy for these sequences formed by a generation, and how can it be become valid for a single generation?[7]

The times of one generation and research approaches

The formation of one generation is, in the first place, a formation of time perspectives. People of one generation have a biographical and historical time perspective in common – or, more precisely, they view their own historical experience from the same biographical perspective. This collectively shared time perspective can be elaborated on three levels.

First, we may consider a more or less objective timetable of the lifecourse which is shared by a generation. The particular structure of the life-timetable can also differ between generations which are produced by historical processes. One way of analysing the objective timetable of generation is through the cohort approach. Here it is interesting to observe cohort-specific patterns of the lifecourse, especially at what point, or age, the transition from youth to adulthood takes place. The appropriate way to do this is to collect life-event data and analyse them on an individual level.

Second, we should consider the dramatic time perspective of the particular biographical script of a generation. Events are followed by people's experiences of them, but people also evaluate their experiences; so that the sequenced experience becomes a kind of drama. A generation's experiences of childhood are relevant as well as their experiences in 'adolescence'. But much more important is the way in which people, looking back, interpret and reinterpret their experiences of the sequence of life phases. The decisive feature here is the form in which later biographical experiences work towards revising earlier ones. Only through the ways in which people make biographical revisions can we understand the plot (the dramatic form) of generational life stories. In this case, the appropriate research approach is biographical. How do people of one generation deal with the fact that they experience changes in their own life, that they are confronted with challenges in the next life phase, and that they discover new perspectives on their own development through life? The research aims to describe how biographical revisions take place, and how one generation elaborates a dramatic understanding of this process; the way to do this is through the interpretation of (auto-)biographical stories (Bertaux and Thompson 1993; Bertaux 1995; Corsten 1998; 2001).

Third, we must reconstruct the formative time of a generation. This refers to both a 'process' time and a time perspective. On the one hand it is defined by the process of becoming a generation of one's own, the time that is needed to generate the background or the horizon of one generation. On the other hand, this process establishes an 'own time' perspective: the view (backwards) on 'our time', the time of 'our generation' – when we were young together. This formative time can be reconstructed through the milieu approach; the research should look for cultural differences between 'adolescent' groups. However, the aim of reconstructing differences here is to uncover how a common horizon of a shared discourse of symbolic distinctions could emerge for one generation. The appropriate way to do this would be through group discussions and protocols of interaction used with the differing youth cultures of one generation (Corsten 1999b; Bohnsack and Nohl 2000).

Notes

1 Therefore, Mannheim attempted also to integrate differing theoretical approaches, namely the positivist (Comte) and romantic view (Dilthey, Heidegger) of generations. For the specificity of Mannheim's approach as a sociology of knowledge, see Longhurst 1989.

2 The term 'actuality', used in the English translation of Mannheim's article (Mannheim 1952 [1928]: 303), is not really satisfactory; it places too much emphasis on Heidegger's 'Jargon der Eigentlichkeit' (Adorno 1964). The adjunct 'eigentlich' could be translated as 'actual'. In German the noun 'Eigentlichkeit' does not really exist – in English too there is no meaning of actuality in the sense of 'Eigentlichkeit', although this translation would be the only one which would make sense.

3 Coleman (1961) combines the intergenerational question of social/cultural reproduction with the emergence of adolescence. See also his newer works (Coleman 1995) and others following him (Husen 1996).

4 But consider the following argument: although in every generation gender or ethnic differentiations will remain, there will also remain differences between generations of gendered or ethnic groups: for instance, generations of feminist activists (Landweer 1996), or of Cuban migrants in the USA (Hill and Moreno 1996) and Greek or Turkish migrants in Germany (Esser 1989; Siefen *et al.* 1996).

5 Honig (1994) attempted to generalise theoretically the idea of a 'generational ordering of childhood'.

6 Douglas Coupland (1992: 21) calls this 'clique maintenance': 'The need of one generation to see the generation following it as deficient so as to bolster its own collective ego'.

7 From the standpoint of developmental psychology, whether children lack the ability to recount their own life in the form of a biographical narration is still an open question. Habermas and Bluck (2000: 753–55) report that no systematic studies regarding this question are available, but that qualitative studies provide the thesis that younger children (up to the age of 12 or 13) create stories that are not integrated with each other or with their life as a whole.

References

Adorno, T.W. (1964) *Jargon der Eigentlichkeit. Zur deutschen Ideologie.* Frankfurt am Main: Suhrkamp.

Alwin, D.F., Cohen, R.L. and Newcomb, T.M. (1991) *Political Attitudes over the Life Span: The Bennington women after fifty years.* Madison, Wisconsin: University of Wisconsin Press.

Attias-Donfut, C. (1992) Generations et repères culturels. *Loisir et Societé,* 15, 419–35.

—— (1996) 'Jeunesse et conjugaison des temps'. *Sociologie et Societiés,* 28, 13–32.

Austin, J. and Willard, M.N. (eds) (1998) *Generations of Youth.* New York: New York University Press.

Bertaux, D. (1995) 'Social genealogies: commented on and compared: an instrument for observing social mobility processes in the "longue durée"'. In M. Diani (ed), 'The biographical research'. *Current Sociology,* 43, 70–88.

Bertaux, D. and Thompson, P. (1993) *Between Generations.* Oxford: Oxford University Press.

Bohnsack, R. (1989) *Generation, Milieu und Geschlecht.* Opladen: Leske.

—— (1997) 'Adoleszenz, Aktionismus und die Emergenz von Milieus: Eine Ethnographie von Hooligan-Gruppen und Rockbands'. *Zeitschrift für Sozialisationsforschung und Erziehungssoziologie,* 17, 3–18.

Bohnsack, R. and Nohl, A.-M. (2000), 'Events, Efferveszenz und Adoleszenz: "battle" – "fight" – "party"'. In W. Gebhardt, R. Hitzler and M. Pfadenhauer (eds), *Events: Soziologie des Außergewöhnlichen*. Opladen: Leske.

Braungart, R. and Braungart, M.M. (1986) Life-course and generational politics. *Annual Review of Sociology*, 12, 205–31.

Brosziewski, A. (2001) Innovation und Erfahrung: Über Generationen und die Zeit der Gesellschaft. *Moderne Zeiten: Reflexionen zur Multioptionsgesellschaft*. Konstanz: Universitätsverlag Konstanz.

Buchmann, M. (1989) *The Script of Life in Modern Society: Entry into adulthood in a changing world*. Chicago: University of Chicago Press.

Bude, H. (1987) *Deutsche Karrieren*. Frankfurt am Main: Suhrkamp.

— (1995) *Das Altern einer Generation: Die Jahrgänge 1938–1948*. Frankfurt am Main: Suhrkamp.

— (1997) Die Wir-Schicht der Generation. *Berliner Journal für Soziologie*, 7, 197–204.

Clarke, J. (1976) 'The skinheads and the magical recovery of community'. In S. Hall and T. Jefferson (eds), *Resistance through Rituals*. London: Hutchinson.

Clarke, J., Hall, S., Jefferson, T. and Roberts, B. (1976) 'Subcultures, culture and class'. In S. Hall and T. Jefferson (eds), *Resistance through Rituals*. London: Hutchinson.

Coleman, J.S. (1961) *The Adolescent Society*. New York: Free Press.

— (1995) *Rights and interests: raising the next generation*. American Sociological Review, 60, 782–3.

Corsten, M. (1998) 'Biographical compositions in the life-stories of young social professionals'. In J. Markantonis and V. Rigas (eds), *Qualitative Research: New perspectives in human sciences*. Athens: Mavromatis.

— (1999a) 'The time of generation'. *Time and Society*, 8, 249–72.

— (1999b) 'Ecstasy as this-worldly-path to salvation'. In L. Tomasi (ed), *Alternative Religions among European Youth*. Aldershot: Ashgate.

— (2001) Biographie, Lebensverlauf und das Problem der Generation. *BIOS*, 14, 32–59.

Coupland, D. (1992) *Generation X: Tales for an accelerated culture*. London: Abacus.

Döbert, R. and Nunner-Winkler, G. (1973) *Adoleszenzkrise und Identitätsbildung*. Frankfurt am Main: Suhrkamp.

Eisenstadt, S.N. (1956) *From Generation to Generation*. Glencoe, Illinois: The Free Press.

Elder, G.H. (1974) *Children of the Great Depression: Social change in life experience*. Chicago: University of Chicago Press.

Erikson, E.H. (1980) *Identity and the Life Cycle*. New York: Norton.

Esser, H. (1989) 'Die Eingliederung der zweiten Generation. Zur Erklärung kultureller Differenzen'. *Zeitschrift für Soziologie*, 18, 426–43.

Faimberg, H. (1988) 'The telescoping of generations'. *Contemporary Psychoanalysis*, 24, 114–42.

Falardeau, G. (1987) 'Le poids d'une generation'. *Sociologie et Societés*, 19, 153–8.

Ferchhoff, W. (1985) 'Zur Pluralisierung und Differenzierung von Lebenszusammenhängen bei Jugendlichen'. In D. Baacke und W. Heitmeyer (eds), *Neue Wiedersprüche*. Weinheim: Beltz.

— (1997) 'Jugendkulturelle Individualisierungen und (Stil) Differenzierungen in den 90er Jahren'. In W. Ferchhoff (ed), *Jugendkulturen – Faszination und Ambivalenz*. Weinheim: Beltz.

Fischer-Kowalski, M. (1983) 'Halbstarke 1958, Studenten 1968: Eine Generation und zwei Rebellionen'. In U. Preuss-Lausitz, P. Büchner, M. Fischer-Kowalski, D. Geulen, M.E. Karsten, C. Kulke, U. Rabe-Kleberg, H.-G. Rolff, B. Thunemeyer, Y. Schütze, P. Seidl, H. Zeiher and P. Zimmermann (eds), *Kriegskinder, Konsumkinder, Krisenkinder*. Weinheim and Basel: Beltz.

Foucault, M. (1976) *La volonté de savoir. L'histoire de la sexualité*. Tome I. Paris: Gallimard.

Glenn, N.D. (1977) *Cohort Analysis*. Beverly Hills: Sage.

Grauers, A. (1996) 'The young generation speaks out'. *Development*, 1, 87–93.

Habermas, T. and Bluck, S. (2000) 'Getting a life: the emergence of the life story in adolescence'. *Psychological Bulletin*, 126, 748–69.

Hall, S. and Jefferson, T. (eds) (1976) *Resistance through Rituals*. London: Hutchinson.

Hildenbrand, B. (2000) 'Generationenbeziehungen in struktural-hermeneutischer Perspektive'. *Sozialersinn*, 1, 51–66.

Hill, K. and Moreno, D. (1996) 'Second generation Cubans'. *Hispanic Journal of Behavioral Sciences*, 18, 175–93.

Honig, M.-S. (1994) 'The generational ordering of childhood'. Paper presented at the World Congress of Sociology. Bielefeld, July.

Huinink, J. and Konietzka, D. (2000) 'Leaving the parental home in the Federal Republik of Germany and the GDR'. Paper presented at the Workshop on "Leaving Home – A European Focus". Rostock: Max Planck Institute for Demographic Research.

Husen, T. (1996) 'Youth and adolescence: a historical and cultural perspective'. In J. Clark (ed), *James S. Coleman*. London: Falmer Press.

Jaide, W. (1985) *Generationen eines Jahrhunderts. Wechsel der Jugendgenerationen im Jahrtausendtrend zur Geschichte der Jugend in Deutschland 1871 bis 1985*. Frankfurt am Main: Fischer.

Jennings, M.K. (1996) 'Political knowledge over time and across generations'. *Public Opinion Quarterly*, 60, 228–52.

Kertzer, D.E. (1983) 'Generation as a sociological problem'. *Annual Review of Sociology*, 9, 125–49.

Kohli, M. (1985) 'Die Institutionalisierung des Lebenslaufs'. *Kölner Zeitschrift für Soziologie und Sozialpsychologie*, 37, 1–29.

Landweer, H. (1996) 'Generationskonflikte und Sachdifferenzen: das Beispiel Frauenbewegung'. *Transit 1996*, 87–100.

Lang, K., Lang, G.E., Kepplinger, H.M. and Ehmig, S. (1993) 'Collective memory and political generations: a survey of German journalists'. *Political Communication*, 10, 211–29.

Lauterbach, W. (1995) 'Die gemeinsame Lebenszeit von Familiengenerationen'. *Zeitschrift für Soziologie*, 24, 22–41.

Longhurst, B. (1989) *Karl Mannheim and the Contemporary Sociology of Knowledge*. London: Macmillan.

Luhmann, N. (1980) *Gesellschaftsstruktur und Semantik: Studien zur Wissenssoziologie der modernen Gesellschaft*. Vol. 1. Frankfurt am Main: Suhrkamp.

Maase, K. (1995) 'Lässige boys und schicke girls'. In P. Alheit, W. Fischer-Rosenthal und E.M. Hoerning (eds), *Biographien in Deutschland*. Opladen: Westdeutscher Verlag.

Mach, B. (1994) 'Self-direction and authoritarianism under conditions of radical systemic change: intergenerational transmission of values and orientations in Poland'. *Polish Sociological Review*, 4, 323–34.

Macpherson, P. and Fine, M. (1995) 'Hungry for an us: adolescent girls and adult women negotiating territories of race, gender, class, and difference'. *Feminism and Psychology*, 5, 181–200.

Mannheim, K. (1952 [1928]) 'The problem of generations'. In K. Mannheim (ed), *Essays in the Sociology of Knowledge*. London: Routledge and Kegan Paul.

Marcia, J.E. (1980) 'Identity in adolescence'. In J. Adelson (ed), *Handbook of Adolescent Psychology*. New York: Wiley.

Marini, M.M. (1984) 'The order of the events in the transition to adulthood'. *Sociology of Education*, 57, 63–84.

Mayer, K.U. (1993) 'The postponed generation: economic, political, social and cultural determinants of changes in life course regime'. In H.A. Becker and P.L.J. Hermkens (eds), *Solidarity of Generations*. Vol. 1.2. Amsterdam: Thesis Publications.

— (2000) 'Promises fulfilled? A review of 20 years of life course research'. *Archives Européennes de Sociologie*, 41 (2), 259–82.

Mayer, K.U. and Schöpflin, U. (1989) 'The state and the life course'. *Annual Review of Sociology*, 15, 187–209.

Meyer, J.W. (1986) 'Self and the life course: institutionalization and its effects'. In A. Soerensen, F. Weinert and L.R. Sherrod (eds), *Human Development and the Lifecourse*. Hillsdale: Lawrence Erlbaum.

Modell, J. (1992) *Into One's Own*. Berkeley: University of Califormia Press.

Niethammer, L. (2000) *Kollektive Identität. Heimliche Quellen einer unheimlichen Konjunktur*. Reinbek: rororo.

O'Brien, R.M., Gwartney-Gibbs, P., Mason, W.-M. and Kahn, J.-R. (1989) 'Relative cohort size and political alienation: three methodological issues and a replication supporting the Easterlin hypothesis'. *American Sociological Review*, 54, 476–80.

Preuss-Lausitz, U., Büchner, P., Fischer-Kowalski, M., Geulen, D., Karsten, M.E., Kulke, C., Rabe-Kleberg, U., Rolff, H.-G., Thunemeyer, B., Schütze, Y., Seidl, P., Zeiher, H. and Zimmermann P. (1983) *Kriegskinder, Konsumkinder, Krisenkinder. Zur Sozialisationsgeschichte seit dem Zweiten Weltkrieg*. Weinheim and Basel: Beltz.

Pilcher, J. (1994) 'Mannheim's sociology of generations: an undervalued legacy'. *British Journal of Sociology*, 4, 481–95.

Pinder, W. (1926) *Das Problem der Generation in der Kunstgeschichte Europas*. Berlin: Frankfurter Verlagsanstalt.

Pronovost, G. (1992) 'Generations, cycles de vie et univers culturels'. *Loisir et Societé*, 15, 437–60.

Rauschenbach, T. (1998) 'Generationsverhältnisse im Wandel'. In J. Ecarius (ed), *Was will die jüngere mit der älteren Generation?* Opladen: Leske.

Rintala, M. (1962) *Three Generations: The extreme right wing in Finnish politics*. Bloomington, Indiana: Indiana University Press.

Ryder, N. (1965) 'The cohort as a concept in the study of social change'. *American Sociological Review*, 30, 843–61.

Schelsky, H. (1963) *Die skeptische Generation: Eine Soziologie der deutschen Jugend*. Düsseldorf: Diederichs.

Schuman, H., Belli, R.F., and Bischoping, K. (1997) 'The generational basis of historical knowledge'. In J.W. Pennebaker, D. Paez and B. Rimé (eds), *Collective Memory of Political Events: Social psychological perspectives*. Mahwah, NJ: Lawrence Erlbaum.

Schuman, H. and Scott, J. (1989) 'Generations and Collective Memories'. *American Sociological Review*, 54, 359–81.

Siefen, G., Kirkcaldy, B.D. and Athanasou, J.A. (1996) 'Parental attitudes: a study of German, Greek, and second generation Greek migrant adolescents'. *Human Relations*, 49, 837–51.

Skelton, T. and Valentine, G. (eds) (1998) *Cool Places: Geographies of youth cultures*. London: Routledge.

Stiksrud, A. (1994) *Jugend im Generationen-Kontext*. Opladen: Westdeutscher Verlag.

Strom, R., Strom, S., Collinsworth, P., Strom, P. and Griswold, D. (1996) 'Intergenerational relationships in black families'. *International Journal of Sociology of the Family*, 26, 129–41.

Straub, J. (1998) 'Personale und kollektive Identität'. In A. Assmann (ed) *Identitäten*. Frankfurt am Main: Suhrkamp.

Thornton, S. (1995) *Club Cultures*. Cambridge: Polity Press.

Völter, B. (1996) 'Die "Generation ohne Alternative"': Generationstheoretische Überlegungen am Beispiel der nach dem Mauerbau geborenen DDR-Jugend'. *Berliner Debatte INITIAL*, 7, 107–18.

Wensierski, H.J. (1994) *Mit uns zieht die neue Zeit*. Opladen: Leske.

White, H. (1986) *Tropics of Discourse: Essays in cultural criticism*. Baltimore and London: John Hopkins University Press.

White, H.C. (1992) *Identity and Control*. Princeton: Princeton University Press.

Willis, P. (1978) *Profane Culture*. London: Routledge.

Part Two
Intergenerational relations – in and beyond the family

3 The transmission of social and cultural capital between family generations

Peter Büchner

This chapter is concerned with relationships between generations and how they constitute a generational system of shaping life trajectories, especially for succeeding generations. In contrast to more traditional approaches of socialisation, which focus on adult society and investigate mainly transition processes from childhood into adulthood, I will look at generational relationships as a lifelong configuration of successive generations whose respective lifecourses are interwoven in many ways. This kind of research into generational relationships can be considered as an important key to a better understanding of human cohabitation in terms of transmission and in terms of continuities and discontinuities between generations.

Like a photographer I can only present a very specific view of my objective by using a particular camera with a particular type of lens and a particular type of film. Here, I intend to present a view on *family* relationships, or a kind of research programme about the effect of family influences on the destinies of successive generations. I will discuss the question by referring to considerations noted for an ongoing research project at the Marburg Institute of Education.

In an earlier research project on children and childhood I have – together with a team of young researchers in Marburg – investigated the everyday lives of children and young adolescents, concentrating on differing models of parent-child relationships on the basis of differing family resources and family traditions (Büchner 1995; Büchner *et al.* 1998; Büchner and Fuhs 2001). With reference to theories of modernisation, we analysed the implications of what is termed destandardisation and biographisation of the children's lifecourses, which entail both more opportunities and freedom of choice and also new forms of risks and constraints. Like many other approaches in the field of childhood research, our research was inspired by the idea of an intensified advocacy for the child and the value of encouraging the child's agency in parent-child relationships. In contrast to adult-centred views of children and childhood, we were interested in finding out more about opportunities for children, enabling them to seek their own pursuits independently of parental direction and parental control.

We reported on general changes in parent-child relationships (at least with regard to previous generations of children) in terms of more equal power balances in parent-child relationships, and celebrated the modern negotiating child as partly autonomous organiser of his or her own biography together with all the associated positive views on this kind of discursive negotiation between parents and children. Children had obviously managed to extend their positional power, since they were granted more rights of co-determination.

Resorting again to the metaphor mentioned above, as photographers we took pictures from one specific point of view. We were looking at children as organisers of their biographies with regard to the differing degrees of freedom of choice and autonomy of action available to them. We were also interested in the children's position within a changing generational order in which children are said to have more opportunities for autonomous action and independent decision-making with regard to getting their biography organised. Our typology of different modes of parent-child relationships mirrors differing family cultures and describes parent-child communication models with differing framing conditions such as degrees of self-regulation and parental control, forms of release from parental control or specific coping and support networks.

A second look into our case material led us to assume, however, that our approach to studying parent-child relationships as part of the whole range of relationships within a given generational order needs revision. The coexistence of the great variety of parent-child relationships indicates differences not only in generational terms but also in terms of social distinction. Parents favour specific parent-child relationships because, by doing so, they hope to place their children on desirable personal *and* social trajectories. In competition with other families, parents develop distinctive strategies for shaping the life trajectories of their children with higher or lower degrees of self-regulation and parental control. Children themselves also act in competition with each other. They negotiate with their parents, not only in generational but also in social (or gender) terms.

The fear of not being able to keep up with other peers or of losing social prestige within the peer group can obviously be a strong incentive for negotiating with parents. If, however, in the process of this negotiating, the need for what Elias would call farsightedness in civilised behaviour patterns is neglected, a biography-related decision might, in the long run, lead to a dead end. Owing to differing coping and support strategies in differing family cultures, some biographical options can obviously turn out to be positive in one family and negative in another.

Lars Dencik (1995) describes, in the context of what he calls dual socialisation settings, the complexity of negotiating and carrying out decision-making processes in private and public arenas and the risk of failure in such different fields of social interaction. His conclusion, which can also be applied to other frames of reference, is that the specific interactional logic needs to be unravelled with regard to very different framing conditions.

I will not go into further details here, but will start from the assumption that we can find, in the social space of a given society (in the sense employed by Bourdieu 1984), distinctive notions of generational order which are permanently translated into distinctive family ways of life and family strategies of interaction yet to be explored. Therefore I suggest that, firstly, we should combine a generational perspective with a one of social inequality or social inclusion/exclusion. This allows us to identify the rules of the game of generalised social competition with regard to specific distinctive relationships between generations whose outcomes permanently shape the life trajectories of successive generations in various – that is, distinctive – ways.

Many approaches within the field of the sociology of childhood pay no attention to the wider social network of family-related intergenerational relationships. The important role of grandparents, for example, is ignored in most approaches. Yet the contribution of grandparents to shaping the life trajectories of their grand-children seems to be of growing importance, since a growing number of employed mothers rely on support by grandmothers. Therefore I suggest secondly that a multigenerational perspective should be taken.

In addition, the following up of children's lifecourses into adulthood is very often neglected, so that we cannot really find out much about successful or unsuccessful lifecourses and their respective framing conditions. Therefore I suggest thirdly that a longitudinal perspective is important. In particular, groups of marginalised children are often left out of consideration. It is important, however, to include risk biographies of children (Büchner 1998) – that is to say, we should not overlook the specifically framed biographical decision-making processes of children who report on problems in mobilising sufficient personal and family resources in support of autonomous negotiating and decision-making about alternative biographical options.

All such shortcomings of research taken together call for a research approach which includes a longitudinal perspective and looks at a wider family network context, with the family as its main window of observation. Rauschenbach (1998) has systematised the study of generational relationships in a typology showing different windows of observation (see Table 3.1, page 75).

I am asking here for a diachronous perspective which allows for insights into the family and the study of family-related lifecourses in successive generations. Such a view is suggested in our most recent research project, which analyses the transmission of cultural and

Table 3.1 *Typology of generational relationships*

| | Micro-perspective | | Macro-perspective | | |
	Actor's view	Observer's view	Actor's view	Observer's view	
Synchronous perspective	my sister, my friends	siblings, peers	my generation	the post-war generation	*Intra-generational*
Diachronous perspective	my mother, my son	grandparents, parents, children	the generation of our grandparents	generational change	*Inter-generational*
	Person-to person relationships		Group relationships		

Source: Rauschenbach (1998)

social capital between family generations in a transgenerational perspective (Büchner *et al*, 2003). I propose a longitudinal family-based approach investigating the question of how specific family traditions and family cultures influence, in the long run, the life trajectories of successive generations. With the help of a generational approach of this kind it is possible to look into the dynamics of intergenerational family relationships and the processes of handing down family traditions to the next generations. Since different families have very different family histories and family traditions, our project will try to compare different and distinctive family micro-cultures which can be seen as vital social spaces providing both potential opportunities and potential constraints for its members.

This research is still in its infancy. The project is funded by the German Research Council and concerned with the study of negotiating and interchange processes about the nature and cultural significance of family traditions between generations. In this research project we refer to family as a social network of individuals related by kinship and including three or more generations. We intend to study 'social genealogies' (Bertaux 1995) by investigating family micro-cultures and processes of transgenerational transmissions in order to identify, describe and understand how family resources are used for the shaping of lifecourses in different generations. This relational approach is used by oral history and lifecourse researchers. Apart from occupational inheritance (such as father-son upward/down-ward social mobility) we also cover social and cultural inheritance (continuities/discontinuities in family biographies), which will be observed within the family context. Thus the effects of social change on children and childhood will be studied by investigating family cultures and the changing quality of transgenerational relationships within the family from one generation to the next. Social and cultural capital are thus viewed as family resources with a changing transmissibility. In another research context this topic is discussed under the headline of 'culturalisation of social inequality' (Berger 1995; Berger and Vester 1998), which implies that we should also take into account the rules of generalised intra- and inter-family competition in given social and cultural contexts of transmission in a generational perspective.

The family is, in this sense, providing vital social space for the shaping of life trajectories of all its members, not only the younger generation. In any family network, the pull of family ties can create potential opportunities which enable a specific life trajectory as well as potential constraints or limitations that prevent the fulfilment of life chances provided through given family resources. Therefore it will be necessary to find out more about the mechanism of how individual life trajectories are both conceived and achieved within the family context in succeeding generations. The outcome of transmis-sion processes in relation to their framing conditions can be studied in lifecourse reports. In our project we investigate such questions with the help of intensive family case studies and interviews with family members including 16-year-old children, their parents and grandparents. We use different methods (narrative and focused interviews, group discussion technique, family photo analysis), and we are in some ways obliged to the theoretical sampling approach of Glaser and Strauss (1965).

As mentioned previously, special attention will be given to problems related to social inequality as well as to social and cultural distinction. Distinction has to do with social and cultural boundaries giving or preventing access to both material and immaterial resources (such as knowledge or formal education). Distinction is also related to different modes of inclusion and exclusion with regard to both the generational and the social structure of a given society. It is necessary to find out which strategies are thought to be successful in order to be distinctive and which channels are being used by family members to mobilise various kinds of family resources in order to remain both up to date and competitive with other families. It is also necessary to ask how family cultures are changing in succeeding generations. To summarise, we will examine the continuities and discontinuities of family traditions in different family cultures in succeeding generations.

Childhood research has been criticised for the familialisation of children and childhood – the reduction of children to their role within a parent-child relationship in an essentially private institution (the family). However, in developing our generational approach, we started from the assumption that family traditions and different family cultures are still central reference points for understanding the modes of production and reproduction of all sorts of capital in succeeding generations. This applies to the production of human capital and its macro-sociological implications as well as to the production of social and cultural capital (in the sense used by Bourdieu 1986) and its person-related micro-sociological implications. I am referring especially to social and cultural capital, which is produced and reproduced in and by children through their activities and their efforts in learning both inside and outside of school. In the family context this happens in the course of transmission and negotiating processes influenced and controlled by family members both in its organisation and in its contents. Thus we are interested in the creation and preservation of social and cultural capital in the minds and bodies of succeeding generations within the family context.

On the one hand, it is true, we are confronted with a process of defamilialisation of the modern child. A number of studies indicate a decreased intensity of family-centred life and, simultaneously, an increase in control over the child's relationship with adults by professional childworkers outside the family context. Close family ties and direct control of children's everyday lives through the parental home seem to be at least in part delegated to and replaced by leisure institutions, peer group and media influences. It has frequently been argued that there is a trend towards a diminution of the role of the family in general and especially with regard to cultural transmission and socialisation.

On the other hand, in spite of this recognition of the importance of professionals (for example, teachers or staff in scholarised leisure institutions), or even non-professional childminders, in the experience of children themselves, there is the danger of underestimating the family's influence on the shaping of life trajectories of successive generations. It seems to be a strong 'modern' tendency to undervalue and even delegitimise the family as a channel of transmission. The supposedly growing importance of out-of-home education seems to support this view. But educationalists' and politicians' desire to compensate for shortcomings in the field of (private!) family socialisation by delegating important elements of education to public childwork institutions has turned out to be, in many respects, an illusion. The German discourse on whole-day schooling mirrors the problems inherent in such lines of thought.

Even if it is not generally true, as Oldman (1994: 56) assumes, that 'the quality of life enjoyed by adults is enhanced by their control over the process of growing up ... and that the quality of life for children, as they grow up, is thereby reduced', we have to be aware of the complexity of this trend towards a decreasing involvement of parents in the business of bringing up children. Out-of-family childwork is predominantly middle-class work and, at the same time, middle-class families benefit disproportionately from its provision (ibid: 58). In particular, middle-class children are being 'childworked' on in a very different way: different programmes, different standards and different participation rates show structures of social inclusion and exclusion which cannot be ignored.

Therefore it is necessary to combine a generational research perspective with a perspective open to insights into the family-related modes of reproduction of social inequality and modes of both generational and social exclusion. Despite the tendency towards more market-based opportunity structures for children, we have to take into account the long arm of family traditions and family resources (both material and immaterial) which play a crucial role with regard to the shaping of life trajectories of successive generations not only in generational terms but also in terms of social inequality.

Research on inter-generational relationships has its own tradition and cultural semantics. From an educational point of view, we take it for granted that children must be integrated into society and supported by educational transmission processes between the generation of parents educating and teaching the child and the young generation being educated and taught by parents and other adults. The parental generation is, in this sense, the agent of cultural reproduction.

After discovering the child as an active person in his or her own right, we are now accustomed to consider additionally the child as a particular unit of observation. In making the transition from being a child to being an adult, children are seen as agents in their own construction, working at their vocation of becoming adult. The notion of the child as actor and constructor in his or her own right takes account of the asymmetrical power relationships between the older and the younger generation. But at the same time the sociology of childhood must be open to consider power relationships in terms of gender and the structure of social inequality. The concept of transmission can help to understand such complex interrelationships.

Writing for an English audience – including those working at the Institute of Education, University of London – about transmission, and especially about cultural transmission, is like carrying coals to Newcastle. Basil Bernstein is of course well known for his research on transmissions between generations. His theory of (cultural) codes portrays principles of social and cultural differentiation and lays open the mechanisms of the reproduction of social inequality in a changing society. His work is most suitable for comprehending the relationships between social class, culture and socialisation. Bernstein 'looks at four elements in the social process: first, the system of control; second, the boundaries it sets up; third, the justification or ideology which sanctifies the boundaries; and fourth, the power itself which is hidden by the rest. The analysis always ends by revealing the distribution of power' (Douglas 1972: 312). Bernstein (1974) talks about children as clients of the educational system and specifies modes of cultural experience, mediated through the codes, which are peculiar to certain groups of children and which can also help to understand the social construction and reproduction of childhood within the family and the early years of schooling.

Schooling and the reproduction of different bodies of knowledge and schools as agencies of cultural reproduction are topics that are associated with Bernstein's work. With reference to Durkheim he claims that, in principle, contemporary schools are in a process of transition from social arrangements founded upon and manifest in mechanical solidarity (with ascribed pupils' roles) to those associated with organic solidarity (with the establishment of achieved pupils' roles) (cf. Atkinson 1985). Here we find parallel developments to the modern family, since the family-based communication model of negotiation is guided by similar norms and values. The study of the family and the process of cultural reproduction belongs in this context. Bernstein's approach is intended both to portray the mechanisms whereby particular social forms are reproduced and to capture time processes of transformation and change. In particular, he strives to unravel the power-related principles of social differentiation, leading to very different consequences for the social placement of individuals.

With regard to family socialisation, Bernstein claims that the modern middle-class mother is central to the work of cultural transmission: she is a carrier of symbolic property from one generation to the next. The variety of family cultures is characterised in terms of more open or more closed role systems, and contrasting family types are considered as different types of communication systems. On the one hand, we find positional modes of authority and control (with the ascribed characteristics gender, age or generation); on the other hand, more open person-oriented modes of conduct are regulated through discussion and negotiation. Bernstein is mainly interested in cultural patterns in human living together as representations of power. So he seeks in particular to uncover the (open and hidden) rules of competition and the underlying principles of transmission (and transformation) of such cultural patterns, which he terms codes and which are principles of selection and a combination of cultural elements constituting specific family cultures. In this sense, codes are culturally determined positioning devices which position subjects within the system of social inequality and, I would like to add, within the generational structure of society. In our own research project we will follow Bernstein's concept in so far as we are also interested in principles of transmission within the family context. By using the terms cultural and social capital we are following in another respect the work of Bourdieu, who is preoccupied with the structure of family cultures and their principles of distinction.

In terms of transmission, it is important to note that a family does not necessarily live together in a common household. In our own research, we allow for different kinds and quality of relationships within the family context, which may even include or exclude different members for different reasons. Our so-called transgenerational perspective is open to the observation of family histories and the development of family cultures covering at least three generations: grandparents, parents and grandchildren. Our investigation of the transmission of common life experience, and especially of cultural and social capital over several succeeding generations, is inspired by, among others, the Anglo-French empirical research project 'Families and Social Mobility' by Daniel Bertaux (Paris) and Paul Thompson (Essex), which is very much concerned with transmission processes over three and more generations within families and the social inheritance of various forms of capital (cf. Bertaux and Thompson 1993). The Yearbooks of Oral History and Life Stories document many of the results of this research tradition (cf. also Bertaux and Bertaux-Wiame 1991).

Until quite recently, transmissions between older and younger generation have traditionally been of central interest for researchers investigating adult-child relationships for educational reasons. Schleiermacher's famous question (1957), asked from an education-alist point of view ('What does the older generation want of the younger generation?'), indicates the social logic behind this kind of approach. Inter-generational relationships are, in this tradition, discussed with reference to family education and family socialisation, and are seen – as already mentioned – in a dualistic perspective as a binary system of inter-generational relationships between old and young, with the older generation as transmitter of basic norms and practices such as language, religion or cultural habits.

In contrast to the underlying assumption of this (traditional) conceptualisation of inter-generational relationships we find, in empirical research, some evidence which does not entirely support this view. In youth research Böhnisch (1994: 112) identifies a pragmatic co-existence of generations to replace the old model, which insisted primarily on the notion of generational conflict. He identifies a shift in the balance of power between generations, with an older generation no longer insisting on strictly hierarchical relationships but open for the idea of a generational contract. We are experiencing, it is argued, a new debate about the shaping of generational contracts, with a change in conflict and competition patterns, new elements of negotiation between generations and more opportunities of participation for successive generations. Zinnecker (1997) also argues in favour of a revision of the binary pedagogic code, maintaining that we should at last recognise the increasing existence of three-generation networks with new forms of educating, caring and supporting practices.

In gerontological studies we find additional evidence for the observation that, in many respects, the older generation's practical experiences and skills have become obsolete as the pace of social change quickens. Parents also seem to find their life experiences, skills and moral views time and again redundant; and children seem frequently to be left on their own, constituting their own culture and teaching each other and often even their parents (and teachers) too: new skills and values, new ways of living are thus propagated by the young generation and adopted by the adult generation. With reference to Margaret Mead's three-stage model of societal development (Mead 1971) we seem, in this sense, to live no longer in a post-figurative society but rather in a co-figurative and, increasingly, a pre-figurative world.

Yet there is at the same time clear evidence that Margaret Mead was mistaken. The older generation remain in power politically and economically and the consumer markets are by no means controlled by the young. Mead's misunderstanding arose from her failure to distinguish the coexistence of many different channels of transmission (Bertaux and Thompson 1993: 5). Challenges to parental authority were certainly important and reflected important changes. But the diminution of the role of the family in terms of cultural transmission and the socialisation of children describes at least an ambivalent development. On the one hand, we are observing a growing number of mothers entering the labour market and calling on pre- and after-school childcare services outside the family; we find high rates of children attending out-of-school classes or other formal leisure activities which open up out-of-family environments and social relationships; and we find a low level of family commitments and family time among the young, which is a gain of time spent with the peer group. All this contributes to children's experience of conflicting adult attitudes and habits, with related normative implications.

On the other hand, it is an open question whether other adults really have co-parenting functions. And in terms of transmission of cultural and social capital, the family (including parents and grandparents) certainly plays an important role, even if we take into account the pathologies which seem to be inherent in family-related influences and processes of cultural and social transmission. The outcome of a child's educational career depends equally on formal education and trans-generational family culture – which is yet to be investigated. Individual biographies (not only of children) are influenced by family biographies – that is, the family dynamic over more than two generations. Despite many other forms of access to knowledge, the family's social control function is, so we assume, not yet obsolete. On the contrary, the family is an important channel of transmission of social and cultural capital. What we need is empirical research with a design not restricted to the traditional generational perspective, which is mostly dualistic (adult-child relationships as a binary system). This would allow for the observation in some depth of the long cycles of (three or more) generations succeeding each other and transmitting social and cultural capital.

References

Atkinson, P. (1985) *Language, Structure and Reproduction*. London: Methuen.
Berger, P. (1995) 'Lebensstile – Strukturelle oder personenbezogene Kategorie?' In J. Dangschat and J. Blasius (eds), *Lebensstile in den Städten*. Opladen: Leske and Budrich.

Berger, P. and Vester, M. (1998) *Alte Ungleichheiten – Neue Spaltungen*. Opladen: Leske and Budrich.

Bernstein, B. (1974) *Class, Codes and Control*. London: Routledge and Kegan Paul.

Bertaux, D. (1995) 'Social genealogies: commented on and compared: an instrument for observing social mobility processes in the "longue durée"'. In M. Diani (ed), 'The biographical research'. *Current Sociology*, 43 (2), 70–88.

Bertaux, D. and Bertaux-Wiame, I. (1991) 'Was du ererbt von deinen Vätern ...'. *BIOS*, 4, 13–40.

Bertaux, D. and Thompson, P. (1993) *Between Generations*. Oxford: Oxford University Press.

Böhnisch, L. (1994) *Gespaltene Normalität*. Weinheim and München: Juventa.

Bourdieu, P. (1984) *Distinction*. London: Routledge and Kegan Paul.

— (1986) 'The forms of capital'. In J. Richardson (ed), *Handbook of Theory and Research for the Sociology of Education*. New York: Greenwood.

Büchner, P. (1995) 'The impact of social and cultural modernisation on the everyday lives of children'. In M. du Bois-Reymond, R. Diekstra, K. Hurrelmann and E. Peters (eds), *Childhood and Youth in Germany and The Netherlands*. Berlin and New York: de Gruyter.

Büchner, P. (1998) '"Die woll'n irgendwie nich". Wenn Kinder keinen Anschluss finden' ['If children cannot keep up with other peers']. In P. Büchner, M. du Bois-Reymond, J. Ecarius, B. Fuhs and H.-H. Krüger (eds), *Teenie-Welten. Aufwachsen in drei europäischen Regionen*. Opladen: Leske and Budrich.

Büchner, P., du Bois-Reymond, M., Ecarius, J., Fuhs, B. and Krüger, H.-H. (1998) *Teenie-Welten. Aufwachsen in drei europäischen Regionen*. Opladen: Leske and Budrich.

Büchner, P., Brake, A., Krah, K., Kunze, J. and Merte, I. (2003) *Familiale Bildungsstrategien als Mehrgenerationenprojekt*. Online. Available HTTP: < http://staff-www.uni-marburg.de/~fambild/ > . Accessed 5 June 2003.

Büchner, P. and Fuhs, B. (2001) 'Children are schoolchildren: relationships between school children and child culture'. In M. du Bois-Reymond, H. Sünker and H.-H. Krüger (eds), *Childhood in Europe*. New York: Peter Lang.

Dencik, L. (1995) 'Modern childhood in the Nordic countries: dual socialisation and its implications'. In L. Chisholm, P. Büchner, H.-H. Krüger and M. du Bois-Reymond (eds), *Growing Up in Europe*. Berlin and New York: De Gruyter.

Douglas, M. (1972) 'Speech, class and Basil Bernstein'. *The Listener*, 9 March.

Glaser, B.G. and Strauss, A.L. (1965) *The Discovery of Grounded Theory: Strategies for qualitative research*. Chicago: Aldine.

Mead, M. (1971) *Der Konflikt der Generationen*. Freiburg: Herder.

Oldman, D. (1994) 'Adult-child relations as class relations'. In J. Qvortrup, M. Bardy, G. Sgritta and H. Wintersberger (eds), *Childhood Matters: Social theory, practice and politics*. Aldershot: Avebury.

Rauschenbach, T. (1998) 'Generationenverhältnisse im Wandel'. In J. Ecarius (ed), *Was will die jüngere mit der älteren Generation?* Opladen: Leske and Budrich.

Schleiermacher, F.E. (1957) 'Pädagogische Schriften'. In E. Weniger and T. Schulze (eds), *Die Vorlesungen aus dem Jahre 1826*. Vol 1. Düsseldorf and München: Küpper.

Zinnecker, J. (1997) 'Sorgende Beziehungen zwischen Generationen im Lebensverlauf'. In D. Lenzen and N. Luhmann (eds), *Bildung und Weiterbildung im Erziehungssystem*. Frankfurt: Suhrkamp.

4 Generation and gender: childhood studies and feminism

Berry Mayall

This chapter explores links between the social condition of women and of children, and argues for conceptualising intersections of generation and gender. Though it is understandable that, in general, feminists from the 1970s onwards have not taken account of the social study of childhood, proper understanding of the social order requires that they do so. I am arguing that the study of the division of labour must take account of children's contributions, and that these contributions are importantly mediated through children's relations with women, especially with mothers. Furthermore, if childhood is defined in contra-distinction to adulthood, there has to be a two-way process of definition and redefinition. If we move towards rethinking childhood, this must lead us to rethink adulthood, and in particular motherhood (see Alanen 1992: 64–71).

Feminism and childhood studies

As a preface to the discussion of children's relations with women, we do of course have to recognise that no matter what changes in the social status of women have occurred, and regardless of the particular society being discussed, it is with women that children have the strongest relations. The gender order decrees that women are responsible for childcare and education, at least during the early years of childhood. Additionally, it is women who are expected to run households, provide the food, do the cleaning (even in 'advanced' Nordic countries); and to juggle those responsibilities with paid work. As children's first carers, women form strong bonds with their children, as is shown when parents split up: subsequently, children mostly live with their mothers.

Second-wave feminism from the 1970s onwards has worked with the concept of gender in order to critique and deconstruct inequalities in social status between men and women, between boys and girls. Feminists have pointed to the structuring force of gender in all areas of political, social and personal life. Women's lives have traditionally been structured by child-bearing and childcare, both ideologically and in practice; and the feminist equality project has worked towards more equal sharing of childcare with men and with the state. In identifying societal assumptions that mothers should take primary responsibility for childcare as a principal stumbling block to women's emancipation, women have indeed focused on a key issue. But in so doing they have simplified child-adult relations to a degree that distorts their analysis and fails to give due theoretical recognition to the actualities and complexities of women's relations with children both in early childhood and throughout the lifecourse.

The formulation on which feminists drew – children as 'becomings', as socialisation projects in a preparatory stage of life in an asocial or private domain – was a component of mainstream sociological structures in the 1970s. Early reviews of feminist writings (Ramazanoglu 1989; Leonard 1990) indicate an adult-only focus in feminism, with a few notable exceptions where age as well as gender feature. But the sociology of childhood has been developing since the 1980s, and there is now a solid body of work. For the purposes of this paper, it is enough to point to two principal features of the analyses in this work. Childhood is understood as a constituent part of a generational order, and seen as a social status that plays its part in the division of labour. And children are understood as social agents who are active in relations, with adults and children, and who work on the project of their own life. Within this understanding, it is relevant to explore the idea of children as constituting generation groups.

However, recent feminist accounts from the English-speaking world indicate no influence or very few influences from sociological work on childhood. Time and again, the index in feminist books refers to children and childhood only under 'childcare', or sometimes 'child abuse'; that is, children are understood as objects of adult activity. Generally, feminists of all persuasions do not discuss childhood, but emphasise mothers' childcare work. Thus for Lynne Segal (1995), who reviews the stages of feminist work, the central issue is the status of women and how this can be improved; adult gender relations are the topic. Feminist analyses of 'the family' also focus almost exclusively on adult gender relations, adult paid work and childcare responsibilities (for instance, Bacchi 1999; Bryson 1999). Harriet Bradley's study (1996) recognises age as a neglected variable in stratification studies, and childhood as a lifecourse stage; but she takes the matter no further, preferring to focus on youth and old age as interesting arenas for discussion. Feminist studies of educational issues identify gender as the fundamental underlying concept through which experience, process and outcome may be understood.

Children and childhood did feature as topics of interest for feminists – albeit minor or marginal ones – in the 1980s, in discussions of patriarchal power over both women and children within 'the home' (Delphy 1984). 'Woman abuse' and 'child abuse' have also been linked. Margaret Stacey (1981) and Dorothy Smith (1988) noted that the study of women's lives must include the study of intersections with children's lives – or, more grandly and radically, that the study of the division of labour must take account of children's contributions – but the focus of their studies is on women's work. More recently Lynne Segal (1999: 206–11) argues that the abuse of women and children within the nuclear family is masked and denied through the Labour Party's support for 'the family', with the complementary rhetoric, implied by Labour and overt in the media, that non-nuclear families – 'fatherless' children, 'divorced families' and 'lone-parent families' – constitute social problems and inadequate 'parenting'.

In seeking an explanation for feminists' neglect of theoretical initiatives on childhood, Chodorow and Contratto, in their paper on the perfect mother (1982), suggest that feminists faced alternatives within current social thinking. Some accepted dominant cultural assumptions about mothering, based on developmental accounts of children's 'needs' for full-time maternal care; if psychologists said children 'needed' maternal care, then feminist thinkers had to define children as 'adversaries' of women. The liberation of women was not compatible, simultaneously, with the liberation of children. Alternatively, feminists might start from role-learning theories about the ways in which girls are taught by their mothers to become acceptable women within current social assumptions about gender relations. Through the workings of the patriarchal order, the mother is forced into pressurising her daughters into conformity. In both cases, the child is passive – 'a passive reactor to drives' (needs) or passive in the processes of socialisation (ibid: 70–1). In their concluding paragraphs, Chodorow and Contratto hint at how feminists could and should rethink childhood – conceptualising children as agents with active capacities for relationships, and studying adult-child relations (not just mother-child relations) beyond infancy. (See also for discussion Alanen 1992: 32–5.)

Perhaps we should take account too of how ideologies under-pinning family policies differ across societies, and shape ideas about women's relations with children. In so-called liberal societies,[1] such as North America, Australasia and the UK, the state provides daycare only for extreme 'welfare cases', and women's battle to win paid employment and career and political engagement is a battle to free themselves from the social assignment to mothers of childcare responsibilities. Feminists think they must push children aside, theoretically and in policy-related arguments, in the interests of advancing women's rights. In social democratic societies in Europe, by contrast, policy measures to support early childcare at home, to provide daycare services after the first year or so, and to encourage fathers to share in domestic childcare, have allowed feminists to focus (relatively) untrammelled on gender issues in adult relations in both the 'public' and 'private' spheres: the continuing gendered inequalities in pay and careers, in political life, and in the domestic division of childcare. Since the state takes responsibility for providing daycare services, parents are relieved of that responsibility during their paid working hours. The interests, including the rights, of children are a separate agenda, dealt with by a different constituency, and by other policies.

In both sorts of society, the division of responsibility for children seems to distract feminists' attention from children as persons and from childhood as social status; children and childhood remain a childcare and daycare issue. In the UK, post-war debates on the 'need' for maternal care for young children raged for over 30 years (see for instance Leach 1979), but have died down somewhat in the last 20 years, largely because policies that impoverished families have resulted in the dire necessity for mothers to bring income into their families (Oppenheim and Lister 1996). Furthermore, governments have encouraged mothers to do paid work, in order to reduce welfare costs. The quality of children's experience during the day has become, politically and socially, a relatively minor matter. By contrast, in many other European countries it has become an accepted fact of life that children will spend most of their days, from their second year, in daycare. This social acceptance of the institutionalisation of young children has reduced interest in alternatives (though it has encouraged some service providers to develop democratic practices in daycare centres). But the societal assumption is that parents will re-enter the labour force after a year or so of leave (Moss 1997).

However, a relatively minor stream in feminist thought has, since the early 1980s, briefly outlined rationales for taking account of children and childhood. Philosophical students of feminism such as Janet Radcliffe Richards argue that children should not be seen as commodities whose care falls on women but whose value is to the society; children should be seen as having rights – and therefore the state should ensure 'that their needs are met' (Radcliffe Richards

1980: 310–17), through providing services and benefits which target children directly (income support, daycare, health, education). Jean Bethke Elshtain (1981: 348) briefly includes children in her discussion of citizenship and participation towards reforms of the social order. Alison Jaggar (1983), discussing socialist feminism, notes its assumptions that people, from birth onwards, engage in self-creation, and that early childhood is a formative time of life. On the basis of respect for children as persons and also, pragmatically, because those persons will be the adults of the future, she argues:

> Taken together, these views suggest that children must be fully active participants in making the decisions that affect them most directly and so participate in controlling their own lives ... Children are smaller and weaker than adults; they are less skilled and have less information. Like adults, however, they create their own nature through their own forms of daily praxis. Both the dignity of children now and a concern for the future society they will construct require that revolutionaries take seriously the notion of extending democracy to children. Of course they should include children in those reflections.
>
> (Jaggar 1983: 343)

Barrie Thorne (1987), a student of both feminism and of child agency, argues for consideration of the complex intertwining of age and gender categories, for deconstruction of ideologies of childhood and attention to varieties of childhood experience, and for full exploration of children as social agents. With remarkable prescience, she argues that children must be regarded as agents negotiating with institutional structures, across private and public domains.

These points are taken up by Leena Alanen in her analysis of 'the child question in feminism' (1992: 26). Her study also analyses ways in which the methods of feminism (critique, deconstruction, conceptual development, standpoint) can be applied in childhood studies.[2] Additionally, her empirical study of children's daily lives in lone-mother households draws attention to their constructive agency in shaping their experience, in intersection and negotiation with their mothers.

These provocative analyses provide the basis for the discussion in this chapter. Like these pioneers, I argue that feminists must take part in the re-theorising of childhood in relation to adulthood, and thus give serious attention to the social status, social positioning and contributions of the various social groups that construct the social order. This requires study of how gender and generation are implicated in structuring the social order.

In this chapter, I start from the sociology of childhood in order to explore these issues. I take up, in particular, what we learn from and about children as agents, and link this knowledge to concepts developed in feminist work to theorise women's contributions to the division of labour: the concept of 'people work', and the idea of the intermediate domain. I consider gender-generation links at two levels – where we consider childhood as a structural component of the generational order and where we understand children as members of a generation group.

Childhood as a component of the generational order

My argument here is that changes in the social character and status of childhood will have implications for the social character and status of women, and vice versa. I think we can see such changes taking place in UK society, albeit more slowly than in some other 'advanced' societies. It is clear, to start with, that women's increased participation in paid work affects how children, including the youngest, spend their days. Being able to support oneself and one's children must also be a factor enabling women to leave unhappy partnerships; again, children's lives will be changed in response. In practical terms, then, women's activities alter children's activities.

These changes can be seen within the context of changing understandings of childhood and motherhood, and can also be viewed as helping to establish changes in understanding. When young children move into daycare, this means, to varying degrees in different countries, that they enter into direct relations with the state, which provides services for them, not as members of families but as persons and as a social group, deserving of appropriate provision. In countries such as Finland, with socialist traditions, children are regarded as citizens in their own right. Although in the UK daycare for under-threes has traditionally been provided as a service to mothers, mainly through the private sector, the state has for many years set standards for daycare, thus accepting a direct relationship with the child population. Nowadays, state interest in the education of its youngest children is developing, to some extent encouraged by the merging of care and education services under the education department (currently called the Department for Education and Skills); school achievement at age five is thought to require state attention to children's educational and social activities at ages three and four. This increased state intervention and assumption of responsibility is part of a more general European movement over the last 100 years to monitor, improve and control children's lives (Therborn 1993).

These developments in the social position of young children – that is, their increasingly direct relations with the state – have implications for the social position of mothers. Even in the UK, we have to engage with a new proposition: that the division of responsibility for early childhood between mothers and the state has shifted. The social character and status of mothers is changing: motherhood now legitimately includes paid employment; responsibility for childcare is (somewhat) shared with the state. There is, however, a time lag, especially in UK political and professional circles: old beliefs cling on, though practices and policies change.

Interrelations can also be identified between the social status of school-age children and that of women. In societies where it is normal for parents to work, children are expected to manage their daily lives competently. Thus, in Finland, for instance, seven-year-olds are expected to take responsibility for getting themselves to and from school, and for organising their time out of school hours. This in turn means that motherhood has specific characteristics. Mothers can be seen in partnership with the state – between them, they provide for and enable children to live independent and competent lives. Motherhood is not defined in terms of total responsibility for child welfare, or in terms of an extremely asymmetrical mother-child relation; rather, motherhood, like childhood, is experienced in a society which respects both statuses and provides for both.

This interrelation between notions of motherhood and childhood has differing characteristics in the UK. Here, alongside the changes noted above, we have continuity. Distinctive adult gender roles remain relatively intact, including the myth of the male breadwinner, and women's principal ascribed responsibility for children and homemaking. UK childhoods are characterised by an asymmetrical relation with mothers; even during their school years children are understood as dependent, immature, irresponsible, incompetent, requiring mothers to protect, supervise, control and educate them. Again, ideas lag behind practice, since most mothers of under-18s now go out to work, and the state increasingly provides for their children (through school and after-school services). There is inherent conflict between the mother as paid worker, and the mother as carrying sole responsibility for childcare.

One of the contributions the sociology of childhood can make to the rethinking of motherhood is to suggest new conceptualisations of childhood: that children are competent, contributing, moral agents; that the perceived need to protect them arises not only from their inherent biological vulnerability, but from socially constructed vulnerability brought about by adult-ordered social environments.

Interrelations of gender and generation have a further dimension. When women move out of 'the home' into public life, their actions not only impact on gender relations, they also affect generational relations. Much of 'women's work' in the public domain is with and for children – in daycare, schools, social services, welfare organisations and so on. Women begin to have some influence in

how adults should behave with children in such settings. More
generally, as women engage in paid work, they bring 'the family'
into focus as a problem, and raise the issue what sort of childhoods
should children have. Notably, in the UK, a few women appointed
to high posts in the 1997–2001 government began to forefront
debates not only on the 'need' for daycare, but also on the more
general issue of the desirable division of parents' time between paid
work and time with children. Through changes in women's social
status, child-adult relations emerge into the public consciousness as
a topic for reconsideration (Therborn 1996).

Rethinking child agency in the division of labour

I have suggested that current thinking in the UK continues to deny
the agency of children, and to construct them as dependent and
incompetent. These formulations can be understood as a denial of
the personhood of children. As Jean La Fontaine (1998) discusses,
social anthropology has been concerned with the concept of the
person in varying societies. Unlike the individual – a material,
biological entity – the person is widely understood as an assemblage
of social roles, and individuals acquire personhood to the extent that
their social roles are recognised and recognised as valuable. Thus, in
some societies, personhood is the result of participation in a public
sphere of life, and so, according to men – who wield the power of
definition – restricted to men. This is a formulation challenged by
women, on their own behalf, and one that increasingly is being
challenged on behalf of children. Children, it can be argued, act
within socially significant, socially useful roles. These activities
include learning, paid and unpaid work and people work.

It has been well argued that children contribute to the division of
labour in western societies through their work in learning; this is the
so-called scholarisation thesis (Qvortrup 1985). While children
formerly worked directly in the labour force, now they are active
in acquiring the knowledge needed to fit them for later life; they

have moved from fields and factories to schools. In the generational order, their contribution is in acquiring education. But here, again, we must tackle intersections of gender with generation, since learning takes place from birth, and much of it in 'the family' – that is, more precisely, with mothers and siblings (Dunn 1988). Basic beliefs about morality are developed in the give-and-take of family life; children are programmed for engagement with moral issues (Kagan 1986) and experience and practice improves their judgment, knowledge and ability to engage in human relations (Damon 1990; Pritchard 1996). It is through their engagement with daily practices and precepts at home that children learn how to maintain, promote and restore their health. It is also through their experiences and actions in daycare and at school that they learn about wider social relations.

Thus children's learning takes place in interaction across the generations, with their mostly female caregivers. The generation-gender influences also run in the opposite direction, since, as has been observed, parents learn from their children to be and to act as parents; in particular, women learn to be mothers.

As to paid work, between two-thirds and three-quarters of UK children do some paid work before the school-leaving age of 16 (Mizen, Bolton and Pole 1999). Recent detailed studies have documented the kinds of work they do, and their motivations for doing it. These include helping family finances, gaining status as proper people, and having some financial independence (Morrow 1994; Chandra 2001; Mizen, Pole and Bolton 2001).

People work

Furthermore, I suggest, in considering children's agency, we should build on the feminist concept of people work. This deals with the problem that much of the work women do – and do unpaid – has wrongly been excluded from sociological study of the division of labour (Stacey and Davies 1983). People work includes the 'interlocking transactions' of service and affection, caring for and caring about, caring as a 'labour of love' (Graham 1983: 28). Hands-on practical caring *for* people, as in household maintenance (providing meals, maintaining physical cleanliness and order) intersects with caring *about* the people concerned: responding to their emotional, moral and practical dilemmas; establishing, maintaining and promoting good relations between people. This notion of people work has been developed to describe women's work, across and within generations; their work is for and on men and children in the family. The notion has also been applied to women's activity in paid work: their skills developed at home contribute to the health of organisations; they tend to work in the 'caring professions'. Caring is the medium through which women are accepted into and feel they belong in the social world; caring is socially understood as a defining characteristic of women (Graham 1983: 30).

Studies of 'ordinary' children's daily lives and activities are showing that children too take part in people work. Studies of children's accounts show that they engage in work across the generations, sometimes in collaboration with parents, and especially with mothers (for instance, Morrow 1994; Mayall 1996; 2002). Children too do household maintenance work: provide meals, keep the home clean. As Anne Solberg (1990) describes (for Norwegian families), women do most of this work, girls some, boys slightly less and men least of all. Children also engage in emotional work; they think relationally, and they participate in the development of good relations within their families. Children tell me that they act as confidants to their mothers and keep up contacts with non-resident family members, such as fathers and grandparents. They explain their childcare responsibilities for younger siblings. At school, children work to acquire and maintain friendships; these are critical for well-being at school, for providing support in an adult-ordered environment, for discussing the wrongs they suffer, and for enjoyment of joint activities and play.[3]

There are also many examples drawn from less ordinary lives: refugee children who, with better English than their parents, help them negotiate daily life in an unfamiliar society (Candappa 2000); children who care for disabled parents or siblings (Burke and Montgomery 2001); children who, faced with parental separation, help to make sense, for themselves and for their parents, of changes in family relations and practices (Brannen *et al.* 2000; Smart and Neale 2000).

It has commonly been suggested that children who care, for instance, for disabled or refugee parents are in some sense stepping out of childhood; they are taking on un-childish responsibilities for adults. In a society which stresses polarisation of social positions – childhood dependency and adult responsibility – such children challenge these stereotypes. Accounts given by these children of their own experiences of service providers' frequent failure to recognise their work and their needs for financial and social support endorse the point (Aldridge and Becker 2002). Yet perhaps we can see these children as acting at one end of a continuum, for longer hours and more intensively, with other 'ordinary' children at the other end, doing lesser amounts of caring.

The intermediate domain

The concept of the intermediate domain was developed to theorise women's work across or between the 'public' and the 'private' domains. Stacey and Davies (1983) argue that women, paid and unpaid, negotiate the status of their knowledge with each other. The example they discuss is a central one in the lives of women: the interactions between mothers and health professionals, such as doctors and nurses, in relation to child health care. Mothers' knowledge differs from that of the professionals; they negotiate with each other in order to arrive at satisfactory working compromises between mothers' experiential, detailed and personal knowledge and concerns, and professionals' theoretical, also experiential, society-oriented knowledge and concerns.

Once we understand children as agents, we can extend this concept of an intermediate domain to negotiations between children and professionals about the status of their knowledge; and to children's agency in moving between the private and the public. For instance, children may deal directly with health services in presenting their experiential knowledge as a factor to be taken into account in discussions between, say, mother, doctor and child. Whilst it has commonly been observed that children are often silenced by adults in such consultations, it seems that respect for the relevance of children's own views is growing. And where serious decisions have to be made, some health professionals do recognise the importance of respecting children's knowledge and wishes, both as a matter of principle and in the interests of a good process and outcome (Alderson 1993). Issues of consent have long been important in the health services in the UK (though less so in some other countries), and children's right to participate in decision-making and consent is a familiar theme (Alderson 2002a).

At school, children's ability to participate in decision-making faces a more impenetrable generational barrier. The social order of the school prioritises adult control. Indeed, in the UK, education policy-making adults do not recognise children's participation rights. They argue that adults, but not children, know what education is for – for the future, and for the wider social good (Jeffs 2002). The status of children's knowledge and of their moral status is lower at school than at home, and their power to make their case is also lessened (Mayall 1999). At ground level, examples are many. It is rare for children to participate in discussions of the curriculum or of the organisation of the school day (Alderson 2002b). On the health front, children may be refused leave to get a drink of water in class time, or to go to the toilet; their explanation for absence from school is not acceptable (a parent must write a note); their sickness bids during school hours are sometimes rejected (Prout 1986; Mayall 1996).[4]

However, children do take part in intermediate domain nego-tiations in relation to school; and I next give two illustrations of how gender and generation intersect. The first example is drawn from a UK study of 'parental involvement' in education, which focuses on how children intervene between the home and the school (Alldred *et al.* 2002). The study took place in the 1990s, when a number of initiatives were designed to bring the home and school closer together: a home-school agreement, which 'parents' are meant to sign, agreeing to conform to school agendas (Hood 1999), and new understandings of homework, whereby 'parents' are supposed to work with their children and to learn through the experience (Cowan *et al.* 1998). There is also commercial pressure on 'parents' (through the publication and advertisement of course books for home use) to work with their children to improve their chances of doing well in standardised assessments.

In the English context, of course, it is mothers' behaviour which educationalists wish to modify, since, as noted earlier, mothers are still held responsible for their children's well-being, and even for their academic success. The 'parental involvement' study found that children play an active part in mothers' involvement, in complex and strategic ways: by initiating, facilitating, accepting; by filtering information from the school; by discouraging, resisting or blocking mothers' involvement. An important finding from the study is that children put high value on the privacy of family life; they value the home as a separate domain from the school; and want control over how much knowledge the school has about them. Thus they play a part in and challenge the school's initiatives to link school with home.

Given that mothers, far more than fathers, interrelate with school and school agendas, it is children's relations with mothers that are affected by these initiatives. The cohort of children currently in school is exposed to new social forces; the children can be described as a new generation, located differently from their mothers, whose school experience differed and who will draw on their memories when assessing these initiatives and when interacting with their children. Thus the personal interrelations between two generations – children and mothers – are mediated by the differing experiences of the two generations.

A second example is drawn from my own study of children's accounts of their childhoods (Mayall 2002: 82–3). The samples included 12-year-old Muslim girls, attending a state secondary school in London. Their parents were first-generation immigrants, and the girls were born in England. Apart from school hours, their days were lived exclusively within the (extended) family; and their mothers closely monitored their behaviour. Mothers expected to check all aspects of homework – what the assignment was, when it had to be completed, that their daughter did it carefully and well, what grade she got for it. Mothers in the extended family compared their daughters' homework grades. According to the girls, their educational success was very important to parents; parents were already discussing what qualifications and career their daughters should aim for, and at what point they should get married. But in order to do well at school, some traditional – gendered – activities had to give way. As the girls told me, Muslim girls at age 12, and certainly after puberty, are meant to take on a major share of housework and cooking, and are also meant to take part in socialising with the immediate and extended family. Commonly the female members of the family will spend a good deal of time together, including eating together, watching TV and visiting nearby relatives. For girls expected both to achieve academically and to fulfil gendered roles, there is potential for conflict over priorities and use of time.

In practice, the girls were able to bring their own knowledge to bear on negotiations with their mothers. They knew, better than their mothers, what schoolwork demanded of them both at school and at home, they also knew how academically able they were, and they had views on their futures. They knew when it was reasonable to argue that homework must take priority over housework or socialising. They thus mediated between home and school agendas. It was noticeable that Muslim boys in this study did not report these complex interrelations between school and home. They too were expected to do well at school, but their mothers (and fathers) did not supervise their activities in this intense way. The boys were freer to choose how to spend time, including doing homework and going out with their friends. They had fewer family social and housework commitments.

The interaction between these girls and their mothers illustrates how, under some circumstances, children and parents may be understood as belonging to differing generations. The girls' stories suggest they belong to differing 'actual generations' in the Mannheimiam sense. They tell of their exposure to profoundly differing sets of social forces compared to those their parents grew up with. A further generational twist is that these parents value transmitting traditional cultural and religious ideas and practices to their children, as well as the benefits offered through the UK education system to their children in terms of status and financial betterment. They are welding together the traditional and the educational strands in their thinking; as some of the girls explained, their mothers wanted them to get qualifications and a professional career, but the career would end with marriage, seen as both normal and inevitable. In contrast to their parents, some of the girls were hoping that education might enable them to delay this inevitable step, at least until they themselves chose. Social contacts at school with other children are enormously important for all children, in providing a forum for discussing social, moral and political issues. For these Muslim girls, their social relations with other girls at school, both Muslim and others, were especially important in allowing them to widen their horizons, intellectually, morally and socially.

These two examples of children's mediation between the home and the school demonstrate intersections of generation and gender in the intermediate domain. In both cases, children used their own knowledge, perspectives and wishes to interpose between teachers and mothers; to counter or modify what the adults wanted, using their own uniquely positioned knowledge; and to make an acceptable compromise between school and home agendas.

Conclusion

This book explores social forces allowing or enabling the formation of a new generation. The examples given above have explored the impacts of, in the first place, educational policy and, secondly, of immigration. As Heinz Hengst discusses, new access to international media is another important social force. And as Pia Christensen and Alan Prout discuss, children may feel themselves to have common experiences as a cohort, through their emplaced knowledge. It is through the study of child agency that these insights are made available, and they contribute to the proposition that the formation of a generation may take place earlier than in 'youth'.

The main purpose of this chapter is to explore ways in which study of the social order may be made more comprehensive by taking account of the sociology of childhood and feminist studies. I have suggested that feminism's analyses are incomplete if they omit children as social agents and childhood as a structural component of the social order. The analyses are incomplete in at least three respects: because they do not reflect the relevance of theoretical developments in the social study of childhood, the ways in which intersections of generation and gender structure adulthood as well as childhood, or the actualities and complexities of women's daily lives with and interactions with children.

I have emphasised that it is useful to study intersections of generation and gender. Child-adult relations can be understood as taking place at the intersections of two interrelated concepts of generation: children as comprising a new, distinctive generation (compared to their parents and teachers) and childhood as a component of the social order, having a distinctive contribution to make. I have tried to approach these issues through studies of childhood, using concepts developed by feminists to describe women's work as contributory to the division of labour. The idea of 'people work' and the idea of the intermediate domain are both useful for thinking about how children and childhood contribute to the division of labour. Much of this work is between generation groups, and between children and women – their mothers, carers and teachers, with whom they interact in alliance, in co-operation, in tension or in conflict.

Finally I note that this chapter stops short of further important dimensions in interrelations between childhood studies and feminism: how these relations develop through the lifecourse. There is a lot of work to be done on how the social status of 'child' and 'mother' changes as people get older. For instance, I am still my mother's child, but our relations changed as we both got older, and were modified by the differing ways in which we worked through our generational position. She experienced childhood and motherhood before the welfare state was ushered in. I was a child of the welfare state and a mother within it. How we worked through our relations was importantly influenced by these earlier experiences. This is a tantalising and complex area for study!

Notes

1 See Esping-Andersen's (1990) analysis.
2 Rosalind Edwards (2002) takes up these points in her discussion of recent trends in the sociology of childhood.
3 There is not space here to explore gender differences between children. However, boys and girls both do people work. Commonality overrides difference.
4 The DFES has recently indicated respect for children's participation rights in education, via a consultation document (DFES 2003).

References

Alanen, L. (1992) *Modern Childhood? Exploring the 'child question' in sociology.* Research report 50. Finland: University of Jyväskylä.
Alderson, P. (1993) *Children's Consent to Surgery.* Buckingham: Open University Press.
— (2002a) 'Young children's health care rights and consent'. In B. Franklin (ed), *The New Handbook of Children's Rights.* London and New York: Routledge.
— (2002b) 'Students' rights in British schools: trust, autonomy, connection and regulation'. In R. Edwards (ed), *Children, Home and School: Regulation, autonomy or connection?* London and New York: RoutledgeFalmer.

Aldridge, J. and Becker, S. (2002) 'Children who care: rights and wrongs in debate and policy on young carers'. In B. Franklin (ed), *The New Handbook of Children's Rights*. London and New York: Routledge.

Alldred, P., David, M. and Edwards, R. (2002) 'Minding the gap: children and young people negotiating relations between home and school'. In R. Edwards (ed), *Children, Home and School: Regulation, autonomy or connection?* London and New York: Routledge/Falmer.

Bacchi, C.L. (1999) *Women, Policy and Politics*. London: Sage.

Bradley, H. (1996) *Fractured Identities: Changing patterns of inequality*. Cambridge: Polity Press.

Brannen, J., Heptinall, E. and Bhopal, K. (2000) *Connecting Children: Care and family life in later childhood*. London and New York: Routledge/Falmer.

Bryson, V. (1999) *Feminist Debates: Issues of theory and political practice*. London: Macmillan.

Burke, P. and Montgomery, S. (2001) *Finding a Voice: Supporting the brothers and sisters of children with disabilities*. Hull: Department of Social Work, University of Hull.

Candappa, M. (2000) *Extraordinary Childhoods: The social lives of refugee children*. Research Briefing No. 5. Swindon: Economic and Social Research Council.

Chandra, V. (2001) 'Children's work in the family: A sociological study of Indian children in Coventry (UK) and Lucknow (India)'. Unpublished PhD thesis, University of Warwick.

Chodorow, N. and Contratto, S. (1982) 'The fantasy of the perfect mother'. In B. Thorne and M. Yalom (eds), *Re-thinking the Family: Some feminist questions*. New York and London: Longman.

Cowan, R., Traill, D. and McNaughton, S. (1998) 'Homework for primary schoolchildren: ideals and reality'. *The Psychology of Education Review*, 22 (2), 20–7.

Damon, W. (1990) *The Moral Child: Nurturing children's natural moral growth*. New York and London: The Free Press.

Delphy, C. (1984) *Close to Home: A materialist analysis of women's oppression*. London: Hutchinson.

Department for Education and Skills (2003) *Working Together: Giving children and young people a say*. London: DfES.

Dunn, J. (1988) *The Beginnings of Social Understanding*. Oxford: Blackwell.

Edwards, R. (2002) 'Introduction'. In R. Edwards (ed), *Children, Home and School, Regulation, Autonomy or Connection*. London and New York: RoutledgeFalmer.

Elshtain, J.B. (1981) *Public Man, Private Woman: Women in social and political thought*. Princeton, NJ: Princeton University Press.

Esping-Andersen, G. (1990) *The Three Worlds of Welfare Capitalism*. Cambridge: Polity Press.

La Fontaine, J.S. (1998) 'Are children people?' In J.S. La Fontaine and H. Rydstrøm (eds), *The Invisibility of Children*. Working papers on childhood and the study of children. Department of Child Studies, Linköping University, Sweden.

Graham, H. (1983) 'Caring: a labour of love'. In J. Finch and D. Groves (eds), *A Labour of Love: Women, work and caring*. London: Routledge and Kegan Paul.

Hood, S. (1999) 'Home-school agreements: a true partnership?' *School Leadership and Management*, 19 (4), 427–40.

Jaggar, A.M. (1983) *Feminist Politics and Human Nature*. Brighton, Sussex: Harvester Press.

Jeffs, T. (2002) 'Schooling, education and children's rights'. In B. Franklin (ed), *The New Handbook of Children's Rights*. London and New York: Routledge.

Jensen, A.-M. (1994) 'The feminisation of childhood'. In J. Qvortrup, M. Bardy, G. Sgritta and H. Wintersberger (eds), *Childhood Matters: Social theory, practice and politics*. Aldershot: Avebury Press.

Kagan, J. (1986) 'Introduction'. In J. Kagan and S. Lamb (eds), *The Emergence of Morality in Young Children*. Chicago and London: University of Chicago Press.

Leach, P. (1979) *Who Cares: A new deal for mothers and their small children*. Harmondsworth: Penguin.

Leonard, D. (1990) 'Persons in their own right: children and sociology in the UK'. In L. Chisholm, P. Büchner, H.-H. Krüger and P. Brown (eds), *Childhood, Youth and Social Change: A comparative perspective*. London: Falmer Press.

Mayall, B. (1994) *Negotiating Health: Children at home and primary school*. London: Cassell.

— (1996) *Children, Health and the Social Order*. Buckingham: Open University Press.

— (1999) 'Children in action at home and school'. In M. Woodhead, D. Faulkner and K. Littleton (eds), *Making Sense of Human Development*. London and New York: Routledge in association with The Open University.

— (2002) *Towards a Sociology for Childhood: Thinking from children's lives*. Buckingham: Open University Press.

Mizen, P., Bolton, A. and Pole, C. (1999) 'School age workers: the paid employment of children in Britain'. *Work, Employment and Society*, 13 (3), 423–38.

Mizen, P., Pole, C. and Bolton, A. (eds) (2001) *Hidden Hands: International perspectives on children's work and labour*. London: RoutledgeFalmer.

Morrow, V. (1994) 'Responsible children? Aspects of children's work and employment outside school in contemporary UK'. In B. Mayall (ed), *Children's Childhoods: Observed and experienced*. London: Falmer.

Moss, P. (1997) 'Early childhood services in Europe'. *Policy Options*, 18 (1), 27–30.

Oppenheim, C. and Lister, R. (1996) 'The politics of child poverty 1979–95'. In J. Pilcher and S. Wagg (eds), *Thatcher's Children: Politics, childhood and society in the 1980s and 1990s*. London: Falmer.

Pritchard, M. C. (1996) *Reasonable Children: Moral education and moral learning*. Lawrence, Kansas: University Press of Kansas.

Prout, A. (1986) '"Wet children" and "little actresses"': going sick in primary school'. *Sociology of Health and Illness*, 8 (2), 111–36.

Qvortrup, J. (1985) 'Placing children in the division of labour'. In P. Close and R. Collins (eds), *Family and Economy in Modern Society*. London: Macmillan.

Radcliffe Richards, J. (1980) *The Sceptical Feminist*. Harmondsworth: Penguin.

Ramazanoglu, C. (1989) *Feminism and the Contradictions of Oppression*. London: Routledge.

Segal, L. (1995) 'A feminist looks at the family'. In J. Muncie, M. Wetherell, R. Dallos and A. Cochrane (eds), *Understanding the Family*. London: Sage.

— (1999) *Why Feminism? Gender, psychology, politics*. Cambridge: Polity Press.

Smart, C. and Neale, B. (2000) *Post Divorce Childhoods: Perspectives from children*. Research briefing. Centre for Research on Family, Kinship and Childhood, University of Leeds.

Smith, D. (1988) *The Everyday World as Problematic: Towards a feminist sociology*. Milton Keynes: Open University Press.

Solberg, A. (1990) 'Negotiating childhood: changing constructions of age for Norwegian children'. In A. James and A. Prout (eds), *Constructing and Reconstructing Childhood*. London: Falmer.

Stacey, M. (1981) 'The division of labour revisited, or overcoming the two Adams'. In P. Abrams, R. Deem, J. Finch and P. Roch (eds), *Practice and Progress in British Sociology 1950–1980*. London: Allen and Unwin.

Stacey, M. and Davies, C. (1983) *Division of Labour in Child Health Care: Final report to the Social Science Research Council*. Unpublished report, University of Warwick.

Therborn, G. (1993) 'Children's rights since the constitution of modern childhood: a comparative study of Western nations'. In J. Qvortrup (ed), *Childhood as a Social Phenomenon: Lessons from an international project*. Report 47/93. Vienna: European Centre.

— (1996) Child politics: dimensions and perspectives. *Childhood*, 3 (1), 29–44.

Thorne, B. (1987) Re-visioning women: where are the children? *Gender and Society*, 1 (1), 85–109.

Part Three
Forming children's identity as a
socio-cultural generation

5 The role of media and commercial culture in children's experiencing of collective identities

Heinz Hengst

Translated from the German by Tim Spence

At a conference held in 1992 to discuss papers for a forthcoming book arising from the Childhood as a Social Phenomenon programme (Qvortrup *et al.* 1994), the Belgian sociologist Wilfried Dumon wondered at the fact that some of the authors, who worked on the programme, were operating as 'rebellious renewers'. To a certain extent, he was ascribing to them (more) sociological imagination when he addressed them as follows: 'From my point of view, you are actors in our society, serving as agents of a new development: the recognition of the child as a person, who has already been recognised as such by industry and commerce . . .' (Dumon 1993: 47).

Other protagonists of the 'new social childhood studies' emphasised that they were well aware that the emergent paradigm is no breech delivery, but rather that social movements had placed the 'childhood issue' on the political agenda and turned it into a topic of public discourse (compare James and Prout 1990). However, the media and consumer goods market – and the discourses it prompts – played virtually no role at all in the establishment of the new childhood research, in the definition of childhood contexts and identification, of the new children, or of their emancipation from 'becomings' to 'beings'.

Almost ten years after Dumon expressed his amazement, at a time when the 'new social childhood studies' have consolidated, dominant concepts still fail to adequately reflect the fact that, with the differentiation of the media world and commercial culture, a childhood discourse has been established that is immensely important for the experience and identity constructions of children. Sonia Livingstone (1998) has criticised the way in which the new sociological child conveys the impression of living in a 'non-mediatised' world, and David Buckingham has stated in this context that, 'Whatever the reasons for it, this approach results in a neglect of what is by any estimate a significant aspect of children's social experience.' (Buckingham 2000: 50).[1] This neglect of a key dimension in the current transformation of childhood is also reflected in prevailing interpretations of inter-generational relations. For all the substantial differences between them, such interpretations have one feature in common, namely the unambiguously binary structure they attribute to the implicit generational order.

Generational differences and socio-cultural change

The media can no longer be viewed as something that can be separated from society, social change and identity formation. It is rather the case that society – and hence also childhood as a social phenomenon, the context to which the experience of children must be related – is continuously defined by individual and collective actors through media in the broadest sense.

The continual expansion of the media, including their manifold fusions with other fields of leisure culture and consumption, necessitates a broad definition of the term (mass) media. A distinction must be drawn between their various technological components: media as channels for conveying messages (for instance, television sets, computers, books as well as toys and diverse accessories) on the one hand, and their semiotic component (language, images, sound codes and other textual and symbolic systems) on the other. To these are added the economic component – the media system as a commercial apparatus. When I speak of the media, then, I am referring to a differentiated, constantly expanding ensemble of old and new media that has meanwhile congealed symbiotically with an entire universe of commodities – especially through comprehensive media merchandising systems. Anyone attempting to analyse such conditions of media childhood must refer to an intricate web of meanings in which children are entangled in many different ways from infancy onwards.

Today's children grow up with and within a world in which media penetrate into every sphere and domain of life. What makes the media a special factor is that they are both non-localised and ever-present. They influence not only the temporal and spatial shaping of everyday life; experience with media products, be they stories, scenarios or characters, leaves its mark in thoughts, in the imagination, in daydreams, entertainments and play. Access to electronic media is difficult to control, which leads to changes in intergenerational relations, arrangements and conditions.

It is possible to study, through their interaction with media and commercial culture, the 'identity work' performed by children in the dimensions and permutations that are relevant today. How people understand who they are, and how they distinguish themselves from others, is associated with the concept of identity. Identity also relates to the way in which people identify with place, or are identified with places by others. Identity is, therefore, the key integrative link between the individual and the social level. As part of our everyday experience in present-day societies, this link has become more difficult to engineer and increasingly fraught with risks. The range of available and traditionally prescribed patterns of identity has shrunk in size within the context of pluralisation, individualisation and destandardisation processes. Identities must be negotiated through communication and interaction, without recourse to any clearly defined scripts.

Given these changed conditions, childhood research must provide a more convincing definition of children as 'beings' – with reference to the dynamic interaction of historical history and life history – than it has achieved so far by the existing theoretical approaches. What I mean by this is, firstly, a stronger (systematic) reflection on the importance of the macro level for the 'everyday, synchronic

experience of the child actually living in the social world of the child'
(James *et al.* 1998: 208) and a more differentiated discussion of the
various aspects of social (and cultural) change that today are
central dimensions of the experiences that children acquire as
collectives.

This brings me to the key concept under consideration in this book,
namely generation. I shall use the concept of generation as a kind of
reference model (heuristically, at most), as a concept with which, in
the 1920s, the interdependencies of individual and social development, and the 'formation of consciousness' of birth cohorts in their
encounters and conflicts with their respective and specific social
condition, were conceived of in new ways. As we know, the person
considered responsible for this development was Karl Mannheim
who, in his famous essay 'The Problem of Generations' (1952 [1928])
broadened the age-old topic of 'intergenerational relations' to
embrace new dimensions, turning it into a macro-sociological concept
where relations between the generations at the community level
(Generationsbeziehungen) become intergenerational relations at the
societal level (Generationenverhältnisse) (Mannheim 1952 [1928]:
288*)*. This was a response to the rapid and all-embracing transformation of modern societies, just as the renaissance of the generation
concept since the beginning of the seventies is first of all a response to
the increasing acceleration and extension of socio-cultural change.

In Mannheim's concept, changing social structure determines not
only the respective *gestalt* and fate of a generation but also the
differences and interactions between the generations living con-
temporaneously in a society. Following Pinder, he termed this form
of coexistence of historical generations 'the non-contemporaneity of
the contemporaneous' (die Ungleichzeitigkeit des Gleichzeitigen)
(Mannheim 1952 [1928]: 283), which is manifested under certain
conditions in the intergenerational transfer of culture. Rapid and
extensive modernisation conditions a growing distance between the
past and the future. Corresponding to this, we witness a shrinkage
or even disappearance of the 'knowledge lead' and advisory

competence enjoyed by elders. The distribution of competencies is being reversed. The future is the business of young people, those who are able to train themselves in the structures and elements of social change relevant for the future, and who are not obstructed by the ballast of tradition.

The common positioning of birth cohorts in the historical stream of social occurrence and the bonds forged by a position that 'certain individuals hold in the economic and power structures of a given society as their "lot"' leads, according to Mannheim (1952 [1928]: 289), to selective perception and processing of world and environment, and fosters a collective 'tendency pointing towards certain definite modes of behaviour, feeling and thought' (ibid: 291). Age groups describe and interpret the world as generations defined by the historical positioning of their youth ('first impressions', 'experiences in youth'). Corresponding self-descriptions and interpretations flow into everyday and public discourses. This is indicated by the usual and commonly accepted terms – generational labels such as 'war generation', 'post-war generation', 'hippie generation', 'stress generation', 'environmentalist generation', 'Generation X' or 'Generation Y'. Demographic metabolism – the generational shifts brought about by the entry of new generations and the exit of old ones – is a fundamental phenomenon of social change and innovation.

One can – with Kohli and Szydlik (2000: 13–14) – draw distinctions between political, cultural and economic generations. Whereas Mannheim focuses in his study (primarily) on political generations, childhood sociologists will probably be most interested in cultural and economic generations. Economic generations are predominantly manifested through common economic opportunities and risks; in this sense, the socio-structural approach of childhood research has identified the transformation of generational differences. Cultural generations comprise cohorts that are characterised by socio-cultural features, by specific '(life) orientations, attitudes and styles', and last but not least by the way they handle media, technology and consumer goods (ibid: 8). This is an area where the new social childhood studies need to catch up with reality. As already intimated, one can apply Mannheim's concept here as well. In the media and in (popular) scientific publications, media and consumer generations are created, with labels being changed at ever-increasing rates. These range from the supermarket generation, screen generation, computer, Nintendo, Tamogotchi and multimedia generations to the net and cyber generation.

It is patently obvious that the common way in which cohorts or age groups use dominant new media or media products is not sufficient to label them as generations. Their members do not operate as collective actors in the public sphere, nor do they develop any specific (common) generational awareness. Nor is there any genuinely convincing evidence to suggest whether (and how) such common participation in media innovations and the like can shape cohorts in any lasting way, and distinguish them permanently from previous and subsequent cohorts.

It should therefore come as no surprise to discover that, in (more) serious analyses of socio-cultural change as a process of mediatisation, there is no fixation on particular media and innovations within media culture in the wider sense. Such analyses show how difficult it is to identify new patterns of selection, perception and processing and to assign these to generations. This difficulty results in a certain extent from the expansion, the manifold fusions, the dynamics and the pace of change in the field of media and consumer markets.

Media researchers and cultural sociologists have tried to identify the new media world and its genesis. Schulze (1992), Kellner (1997) and Baacke (1999), for example, share the common assumption – for all their other differences of view – that the relevant changes in the media landscape commenced in the 1950s and 1960s (thus ushering in a gradual, almost imperceptible revolution). Other authors emphasise that the changes which media and commercial culture have pushed and carried forwards in recent decades have not led to generations that are distinguishable from one other, but rather to the diffuse identity of a new youthfulness. In assessments like this the concept of generation is given up in favour of the model of an age-transcending matter of attitude and behaviour.

Recently, a growing trend towards fragmentation has also been noticed: differentiation, pluralisation and individualisation are on the rise, and bisecting lines of cultural orientation are becoming lost in a multiplicity of foci on phenomena in the media and commercial 'culture worlds' (the duration and stability of which is obviously and noticeably declining, however – compare Baacke 1999: 139). Such a trend raises many questions, one of which is whether generational differences are being overlapped by other differences and markers of the generational order.

A few attempts have been made to elaborate a media/consumer generation profile in more detail. These include a study designed by David Cannon (1994), who worked on the question of what skills, abilities and values those who grew up in a developed media and consumer society bring into the world of labour at the beginning of the 21st century. He identifies a number of phenomena and processes which have especially effected and still effect the establishment of knowledge and values of these cohorts. His enumeration implies invasive media, worldwide consumer products, accessible communication and computer tools, global issues and travel. He is of the opinion that this generation's most common characteristic is not a shared ideology, but sophisticated knowledge of consumer products. He claims that his findings apply to youths of all educational and all socio-economic levels, from those who give up school to the graduate Oxford student. All of them have detailed information about computers, media, fashions and leisure equipment. They enjoy collecting pieces of information, facts, jargon and trivialities. They are lethally afraid of boredom and are extremely interested in learning how to do things. They strive for continued feedback and approval from the outside, are very aware of their appearance and are convinced of the significance of the equality of the sexes, emotional suppression and discretion.

Thinking within the generation concept demands comparisons, not least comparisons which concentrate on the degree of non-contemporaneity of contemporaries, on the differences between the cultures with which they come to terms. Recently the German sociologist Ansgar Weymann's comparative cohort analysis identified cultural generations as (four) technological generations (Weymann 2000). Hugh Mackay (1997) drew up a more comprehensive comparison between the baby boomers, their parents, and their children. However, they have problems in elaborating convincing and exact differences.

In 1998, the 16th Congress of the German Association for Educational Science took place in Hamburg under the banner 'media-generation'. On the one hand, that banner opens up a view of the totality; on the other, it indicates with sufficient clarity – being worded by educationalists – that new ways of perceiving cultural practices, interests, orientations, and so on are difficult to reconcile with what are still widespread concepts and forms of schooled learning. In the foreword to the congress proceedings one reads that educational science is today confronted with a new generation, one that has a much more relaxed relationship with the media than their parents' generation ever had (Gogolin and Lenzen 1999). The expression 'a much more relaxed relationship' is rather bare of content but, more importantly, one cannot consent to the presumed dichotomy that is suggested. The reason is that it is probably very difficult to distinguish, for example, today's 12-year-olds from their 40-year-old parents along such lines as may have been possible 20 or 30 years ago. Culturally speaking, the media have brought the members of different birth cohorts (and some age groups) closer together than they were before. Social change, as all-embracing mediatisation, has caused changes in the relations between generations – and lent greater force to horizontal differentiations. It is virtually impossible to ascribe the drifting apart of cultural styles primarily to generational membership. Above all, school culture and parental culture have long ceased to form an unproblematic (and uncontradictory) unity. The parents of today's schoolchildren also grew up, in a taken-for-granted way, with a highly differentiated media and commercial culture that probably exerted a considerable influence on their interests, their values and their cultural practices. The meaning of the term 'media generation' does not unfold until one relates it to the requirements of school culture, which the organisers of the congress presume to be a specific feature of the generation they are dealing with.

The present differences between generations cannot be determined by labelling today's students as media (or consumer) generation, thus trying to differentiate between them and the generation of their parents. The parents, too, were children moulded by consumption and media – and today they are living in a mediatised consumer culture. What distinguishes them from their children is the fact that they are (in the position of) parents. Therefore, differences between children and parents result from the primacy of responsibility (parents) on the one hand and the striving for autonomy (children) on the other hand. However, since they are themselves media and consumer children, today's parents increasingly look for media- and consumption-based solutions to their parenting problems. The same argument applies increasingly to teachers of their age.

It seems appropriate to me to address socio-cultural change in such a way that differences, power play and negotiations are not analysed with (mere) reference to a two-generational model. The new conditional framework created by the market has provided us with at least three collective forces that influence traditional generational differences and arrangements (compare Hengst 1996; 2000). This new configuration of negotiating collective actors has an impact on the construction of collective orientations and practices, and relativises (reduces) the significance of social relations as generational relations for the experience of being a child today. Growing up in a media and consumer society influences the struggle for identity: identity is gained (partly) through an emphasis on style and image.

Scripting children as media users and consumers

In this chapter, what I am interested in most of all are the traces that socio-cultural change – such as mediatisation and commercialisation – has left and is leaving behind in the collective orientations and patterns in children's conceptual worlds, in their notions of 'us' and 'them'. My interest centres on – to use the term coined by Benedict Anderson (1983) – the 'imagined communities' of present-day children, in order to achieve greater openness for new mixtures in their collective orientations. There is much evidence that the 'imagined communities', especially of younger people, are obtaining new contours through globalisation. And it is a fact not only that the media insert themselves into the constructions of such communities, but also that today's children are growing up in migrational societies, and that many of them gain experience through tourism. However, I am assuming – in view of the omnipresence of the media in the everyday life of children, and given the fact that they (the media) continuously present collectives in distinct and significant environ-ments (members of different nations and ethnic groups, men and women, children, youths, adults and old people) – that this information and these images flow into the collective images of self and others held by today's children from the earliest years on.

Children of today can obtain access to virtually all cultural domains independently of parents and teachers. Media and commercialised culture have revolutionised the pathways for knowl-edge acquisition, and the manner in which children create images of themselves, of others and of the world in general. The consumer careers of almost all children – as well as their experience with places where goods are sold – begin when they are still babies. As soon as children can sit upright in the supermarket trolleys pushed by their mothers, they begin to take an active part in buying activities. If trends are placed in historical and biographical relation to each other, then three significant changes in particular are evident in children's culture as consumer culture:

- an increasing generalisation and multiplication of media and consumer experiences

- a strong tendency towards ever-younger consumers

- a de-hierarchisation of the forms of appropriation typical for age groups.

In the new script centred on market interests, the teleological component, or the notion of further development as higher development and of adulthood as being qualitatively different – an essential element of modernity's childhood project – no longer has any meaning. The new script distinguishes consumers with much and with little purchasing power, with longer and shorter life expectancy, with greater or lesser influence on buying decisions. It sees children as a target group with quite specific needs and interests that are essentially equal in value to those of adults. It is on criteria such as these that the attempts to define children as a market, and to segment them accordingly, are based (Hengst 2001b).

So it is a logical step for James U. McNeal (1992), one of the best-known US experts on marketing to children, to recommend that product planners and developers should live among children to learn to understand what moves them, what they like and what makes them happy. This recommendation is congruent with a common and widespread practice. One aspect that is markedly different from only a few decades ago is that new products are tested on children and youths even before the product development stage. In assisting in this way, young people operate as proto-communities or virtual peer groups. Managers in many sectors of industry work with children and youths in producing toys, computer software and music, in the planning of television series and in the design of internet sites. The deployment of 'trend scouts', 'trend spotters' or 'coolness hunters' is another example of this practice.

Such practices highlight the significance of script change in the biographical perspective. The criterion for interventions into children's culture is no longer a notion of what will give children the capacity to act in the future – as workers, parents and citizens – but knowledge about their current needs, interests and scope for action; it is specific product ideas entertained by children or age groups that are close to them mentally (and) as consumers. As consumers, at least, they are – as Dumon noted – emancipated from 'becomings' to 'beings'. One could characterise the market's script as a double-pronged strategy of adaptation to individualisation. This strategy is based, on the one hand, on segmentation and micro-marketing, but when conducting target group marketing, on the other hand, it also addresses constant factors and on new areas where people share something in common.

Commercialisation of 'imagined communities'

Here I shall confine myself to identifying a few examples which show how children deal with socio-cultural changes by integrating the offers of media and consumer culture into their 'identity work'.

I should like to present quite briefly one pertinent finding of an empirical study I conducted, inspired by an international conference on 'Children and Nationalism' at the Norwegian Centre for Child Research (Stephens 1997; Hengst 1997). The study follows the tradition of those conducted in the 1950s and 1960s into national stereotypes in the minds of children. However, it is more open in defining its key subject matter. The theme of the study is not only, nor primarily, the question of how children view their own and other peoples or nations. The theme concerns the collective concepts of present-day children and their search for the structures and elements that dominate their construction of 'collective identities'. It also deals with children's conceptions of self-identity.

Children in Bremen and Manchester – mostly aged between nine and twelve – were asked 60 questions concerning their views of foreign peoples, their criteria for similarities and differences between these and other significant collectives. Two of the questions were:

Who is more similar, a German (or English) and a French child, or a German (or English) child and a German (or English) adult?

What about a German and a Turkish (or Asian) child? Are they more similar than a Turkish (or Asian) child and a Turkish (or Asian) adult, or a German (or English) child and a German (or English) adult?

(What is meant by the first question are children and adults living in France and, by the second question, children and adults who live in Turkey (or Asia). To prevent any misunderstandings from arising, the interviewers for the second question referred explicitly to this 'reading'.)

The children's responses to these two questions give an impression of how they draw distinctions in their constructions of 'us' and 'them', one such distinction being children and adults. Many children assume a kind of 'Children's International', in the mental sense at least. As far as the first question is concerned, only a handful of children chose a national and thus intergenerational option. Like most German (and English) children, children of Turkish (and of Asian) origin also took the view that there are more similarities between French and German (or English) children than between children and adults from the same nation.

When we asked questions to establish whether children identified more with children from the north than from the south, there was more variation in the answers. Some children took the view that 'children from the south' were qualitatively different from 'children from the north'. Migrant children saw this the most clearly. Some children hesitated, or said that they found the problem difficult. Some children said that children from the north differ from children from the south by virtue of the different conditions in which children live and are brought up. Then again, there were children who did not accept this barrier and who said that children are always more similar to each other – more so, for example, than native and foreign adults.

Some German girls take a more cautious view, although basically tending towards this direction. They emphasise the gender-specific dimension and believe that similarities between girls are less marked outside their own culture. In their opinion, there is a greater similarity between a Turkish girl and a Turkish woman than between European children of both genders and Turkish boys. Their assessment criteria are obviously the different scope for individuality and freedom that they ascribe to the two groups. The symbol they cite as exemplifying the crucial difference is the headscarf worn by Turkish girls and women.

As far as the construction of the 'Children's International' is concerned, it is striking that children push language into the background as an indicator, here more than anywhere else. The culture of children, as evidenced by their responses in this survey, has many languages, including the non-verbal; this contrasts with adult culture. This assessment is partly based on the children's own experience; many (German) children describe how, on holidays abroad, they had no problems understanding children from a particular country or from other countries. One aspect that may be even more important, however, is that they generally assume that children have common interests and mentalities in a way they do not perceive adults to have. They believe that, as a fundamental principle, children have more interests in common than adults, that they are more open, funny, less serious and less kill-joy than adults, and that they are much more prepared to pay no heed to differences between people.

An interesting question in this connection is whether this construction of a 'Children's International', which the children seem to assume, is related to age-specific factors only (they use 'not yet' again and again when making comparisons with adults), or whether there are elements here of a new (generationally specific?) mentality. I would argue that being a child nowadays means growing up with peers and focusing on peers, much more than was the case a few decades ago. Firstly, public childhood arises at a very early stage in children's biographies (kindergarten is now the rule rather than the exception). Secondly, the commercial system engineers communities and common interests, creating peer groups on a global dimension.

In any case, the media preferences and leisure interests of children in the survey exhibited considerable similarities. Our survey corroborates what many empirical studies in this field have shown, namely that all children are fascinated by American TV series and formats, cartoon film, soaps, sitcoms, by MTV and its national adaptations. Asked about their favourite TV channels, the children mention commercial channels only, for example. All children are fascinated by toys and games, leisure and sports fashions that are distributed worldwide. In permanent interplay, the culture industries and peers (as virtual and real groups) put on the agenda what is 'in' at any one time. Many of the children interviewed say that it is important for them to follow trends in the way they dress (with a preference for branded, latest style, clothing and shoes). The media and consumer goods industries do everything to stage children's cultures as peer-group culture, independent from adults. A common, worldwide platform has been created here, and the English language has become a lingua franca. In the sub-cultures of net kids, rollerbladers, streetballers and rappers, the secret codes traditionally created by children are being replaced by American insider jargon.

The children reflect in their 'we'-concepts a common, media-based youth culture that is becoming increasingly globalised. Children and young people make use of global media products in a way that transcends the respective medium through which they are communicated. They follow the topics that interest them in an intertextual way, through television, computer games, comics and the internet.[2]

When the children were asked what it is that fascinates them in their preferred, commercially produced culture, the terms they used most were 'excitement', 'amusing' and 'funny'. And there is no question that they consider such preferences to be particularly typical of children. There is an evident connection, it seems to me, with the demarcations children make from the (imagined) habits and mentalities of adults.

The findings of the study show that the children basically consider intergenerational relations to be a matter of age (thus concurring with the everyday awareness of most people). The 'Children's International' they construct expresses their awareness of a fundamental difference between children and grown-ups that is important to them, and which seems to precede any defined or definable distinction. When they try to specify that difference, however, they very often ascribe characteristics, especially as self-ascriptions, in which the attributes communicated by the media and culture industries are reflected.

In some respects, however, it also becomes apparent that the (collective) age-self is masked by historical and societal elements, in this case by their fixation on consumerism as a way of life. The childhood pattern is blended into the concept of western lifestyle. In this concept, the west is not just a geographical fact. What this means, and how, for example, the criteria for ascribing nationalities to 'us' and 'the others' have changed in recent decades, is shown by the surprising assessment by some children that the Japanese are similar to the Germans, the Europeans, that is, to 'us'. Early studies in the 1960s already indicated a cross-national tendency among children to view western nations as similar (for example, Lambert and Klineberg 1967). This tendency – towards identification with a western lifestyle – is also confirmed in later studies (for example, Werner 1982). Whereas, in the large-scale study by Lambert and Klineberg, the Japanese were characterised by children from western nations as being different, western lifestyle as an orientation criterion has led to present-day children discovering similarities even with the Japanese. This is understandable when one considers the Japanese presence on the world markets for media and commercial (children's) culture. On the basis of technological and leisure criteria, the west also includes Japan. Through entertainment products, such as computers, computer games and martial arts, the Japanese have made a name for themselves.

What I find especially remarkable is the fact that today's children increasingly refer to criteria such as lifestyle, leisure time, media preferences and cultural interests when characterising collective memberships, similarities and dissimilarities (compare Holloway and Valentine 2000). The fact that an important change (of patterns) has taken place becomes evident if one compares these criteria with the criteria stated by children in the 1950s and 60s (Lambert and Klineberg 1967). A similar development can be observed in children's thinking about individual (self) identity.

In addition, it must be stated that the childhood concepts of today's children are, on the one hand, focused on an age group fundamentally different from adults. On the other hand, they are also open. They include elements of childhood as a form of life which exceeds age, generation (in the sense of Mannheim) and nation; however, they also seem to be limited to the western world.

From becomings to beings and back to becomings?

There is much debate today on lifelong learning and lifelong identity work. The tasks facing childhood researchers in the social sciences are, therefore, to analyse – with reference to the macro and the global level – the extent to which children are involved in these lifelong processes. This requires a partial revision (or reinterpretation) of the epistemological break considered constitutive for the new social childhood studies: from the notion of children as 'becomings' to children as 'beings'. Under the current conditions of all-embracing and rapid social change, people of all ages and generations are 'becomings'. In accordance with Leena Alanen (2001) one may differentiate between three different approaches of the new social childhood studies: a micro-oriented sociology, studying active children and their local childhoods; a deconstructive sociology, focusing on the discursive formations of childhood; and a structual childhood sociology, which links 'empirical manifestions on the level of children's childhoods' with their macro-level contexts. It seems important to me – again in accordance with Leena Alanen – not to understand these different perspectives on children and childhood as alternatives, but to integrate them.

Ignoring the macro-perspective, as is especially characteristic for the major part of ethnographic childhood research, makes it difficult to understand the present changes in childhood, children's agency, generational arrangements and generational order. The contributions made until now to a structural sociology of childhood put too much emphasis on categories laid down by industrial society and must be adapted to the changed conditions of growing up – conditions of expanded consumer societies and cultures (Hengst 2001a).

The child as a social construct and generations of young people have changed in accordance with the mediatised consumer culture. In the meantime this culture has become dominant in the western world. This does not imply that all members of society are able to take part in it in the same manner and on the same level. A culture may even be dominant if the majority of people merely strives to participate in it: the predominance can also be identified by the extent by which people express their longings, their hopes and fears, the vocabulary for their motives, self-esteem and self-concepts, (by) using the terminology of this culture.

Notes

1 The reasons for this desideratum in social scientific childhood research have never been seriously reflected upon. My impression is that there is a relationship here to the average age of those who develop the theoretical concepts. What I mean here is that they grew up under conditions in which a relatively uncomplicated media world could still be demarcated with clear-cut boundaries from other social and cultural phenomena – and one could (or indeed had to) have the impression that the most important social issues, including those of the childhood context and the experience of being a child, could be formulated and discussed without having to include the media world in the analysis. Later in life,

as professional sociologists and social anthropologists, they tended, as a result of this conditioning, to treat the worlds of media and consumption rather as marginal phenomena and acknowledged them at best as subject matter for secondary fields of sociological interest.

2 There are doubts about whether children's and youth culture should be separately researched, or whether such a separation should be removed. Recent studies on media reception show that, in certain environments, there are differences in the media preferences and habits of children and young people – though it is the case that traditional boundaries are becoming more diffuse. In this note, I would like to concentrate on a very limited extract from the media and consumption worlds of present-day children as outlined in the foregoing: on media-offers that have been and are used particularly frequently by children, products in which the actors are recognisable as members of collectives, products that children for their part also perceive and handle as collective identity offers. One justification for focusing exclusively this time on the examples I present of television and children's experience with television is provided by the comparative study, edited by Sonia Livingstone and Moira Bovill (2001), 'Children and their changing media environment', which was conducted (between 1997 and 1998) in 12 countries (11 European countries plus Israel) and in the course of which 15,000 children were interviewed.

On the one hand, multimediality, intertextuality and the globalisation of youth culture as integral components of children's media worlds are well analysed in the study, while on the other hand, the role of television as a kind of guiding, age-specific medium is highlighted. Television is the medium most often chosen for excitement and for relieving boredom. What I would like to emphasise, especially, is the central importance of private television channels. The growth of the latter has implications for the generalisation of children's preferred viewing that was clearly shown as far back as the 1980s in an Italian replication study (Bertolini and Manini 1988). In an Australian study children (five to 12 years old) were asked in what age group they would like the heroes in their favourite TV films and series to be. Most children (girls and boys alike) said that they most liked to see people of their own age, somewhat older children, teenagers, or young adults. For the children interviewed, young adults were people around 20 years of age. It goes without saying, after what has already been mentioned about the construction of publics by the media and commercial industries, that – to express it cautiously – there are correlations here. What is worth mentioning is that the interviewed children often found it difficult to give reasons why they preferred these particular age groups. In many cases, they explained their preference for older characters by saying that they acted better, had better roles than children, and usually did 'more exciting things' (Sheldon 1998: 87).

Dominique Pasquier carried out a study of special relevance in this context. Unlike most recent studies on media reception, Pasquier's focus of interest is not on the interaction between viewers and programmes, but on the question how children use television, particularly in order to explore personal and social identities. Pasquier's study related to teenage series, which have become increasingly important in French television since the early 1990s (Pasquier 1996: 351–2). These series, directed at teenagers by the producers responsible, met with huge resonance among their target group, but above all were an absolute hit among much younger children.

These series advanced to become the preferred topic of discussion in classrooms, especially among primary school children. Girls in the latter age group participated especially actively, using the intertextual material in the cult surrounding the series. They engaged in role plays, collected and swapped the merchandise marketed in association with the series and dressed up like their favourite TV characters (ibid: 352). The study shows (based on a survey, on observation, on interviews and on the analysis of fan letters) that the series were used by children 'to explore alternative identities concerning gendered roles and to discuss, within the peer group, the ethic of relationships. The programmes form a sort of neutral and common territory, which helps to reveal one's own position and to negotiate the borderlines of the group's moral values' (ibid: 354). Dominique Pasquier interprets the importance of the series (having recourse to Rousseau's notion of human beings having two births) in terms of romantic initiation: she sees them as the midwife at the second birth, at the transition from one world primarily based on generational differences to one in which gender differences are the cardinal focus. Her interpretation is sensitive to the new challenges that socio-cultural change poses for the children and teenagers of the present: the need to look beyond traditional educational and advisory institutions for models that can act as a guide during the initiation process, in which real and virtual peer groups (the latter older than the former) play an ever more important role. The message – the same one that is communicated by the bulk of the media and commercial industry's offerings – is clear: 'to cope with the new self, friends might help, but not adults' (ibid: 355).

What is interesting is Pasquier's labelling of the topic that dominates reception of the series as essentially one of 'romantic initiation', not least because the dominance of appropriate offerings in the plots, speech and images are the prerequisite for interest in the series extending so far down to such an early biographical phase, a phenomenon that is seen not only in France.

References

Alanen, L. (2001) 'Explorations in generational analysis'. In L. Alanen and B. Mayall (eds), *Conceptualizing Child-adult Relations*. London: RoutledgeFalmer.

Anderson, B. (1983) *Imagined Communities: Reflections on the origins and spread of nationalism*. London: Verso.

Baacke, D. (1999) 'Die neue Medien-Generation in New Age of visual thinking: Kinder- und Jugendkultur in der Medienkultur'. In I. Gogolin and D. Lenzen (eds), *Medien-Generation. Beiträge zum 16. Kongreß der Deutschen Gesellschaft für Erziehungswissenschaft*. Opladen: Leske and Budrich.

Bertolini, P. and Manini, M. (eds) (1988) *I figli della TV*. Firenze: La Nuova Italia.

Buckingham, D. (2000) 'Studying children's media cultures: a new agenda for cultural studies'. In B. van den Bergh and J. van den Bulck (eds), *Children and Media: Multidisciplinary approaches*. Leuven-Apeldoorn: Garant.

Cannon, D. (1994) *Generation X and the New Work Ethic*. London: Demos.

Dumon, W. (1993) 'Childhood matters: a critique'. In J. Qvortrup (ed) *Childhood as a Social Phenomenon: Lessons from an international project*. Eurosocial Report 47. Vienna: European Centre.

Gogolin, I. and Lenzen, D. (eds) (1999) *Medien-Generation. Beiträge zum 16. Kongreß der Deutschen Gesellschaft für Erziehungswissenschaft*. Opladen: Leske and Budrich.

Hengst, H. (1996) 'Kinder an die Macht! Der Rückzug des Marktes aus dem Erziehungsprojekt der Moderne'. In H. Zeiher, P. Büchner and J. Zinnecker (eds), *Kinder als Außenseiter? Umbrüche in der gesellschaftlichen Wahrnehmung von Kindern und Kindheit*. Weinheim and München: Juventa.

— (1997) 'Negotiating "us" and "them". Children's constructions of collective identity'. *Childhood*, 4 (1), 43–62.

— (2000) 'Children's cultures in consumer societies'. In B. van den Bergh and J. van den Bulck (eds), *Children and Media: Multidisciplinary approaches*. Leuven-Apeldoorn: Garant.

— (2001a) 'Rethinking the liquidation of childhood'. In M. du Bois-Reymond, H. Sünker and J.-H. Krüger (eds), *Childhood in Europe. Approaches – trends – findings*. New York: Peter Lang.

— (2001b) 'Kinderkultur und konsum in biographischer Perspektive'. In I. Behnken and J. Zinnecker (eds), *Kinder, Kindheit, Lebensgeschichte. Ein Handbuch*. Seelze-Velber: Kallmeyersche Verlagsbuchhandlung.

Holloway, S.L. and Valentine, G. (2000) 'Corked hats and Coronation Street: British and New Zealand children's imaginative geographies of the other'. *Childhood*, 7 (3), 335–58.

James, A., Jenks, C. and Prout, A. (1998) *Theorizing Childhood*. Oxford: Polity Press.

James, A. and Prout, A. (eds) (1990) *Constructing and Reconstructing Childhood: Contemporary issues in the sociological study of childhood*. London: Falmer Press.

Kellner, D. (1997) 'Jugend im Abenteuer Postmoderne'. In SpoKK (ed), *Kursbuch Jugendkultur. Stile, Szenen und Identitäten vor der Jahrtausendwende*. Mannheim: Bollmann.

Kohli, M. and Szydlik, M. (2000) 'Einleitung'. In M. Kohli and M. Szydlik (eds), *Generationen in Familien und Gesellschaft*. Opladen: Leske and Budrich.

Lambert, W.E. and Klineberg, O. (1967) *Children's Views of Foreign Peoples. A cross-national study*. New York: Appleton-Century-Crofts.

Livingstone, S. (1998) 'Mediated childhoods: a comparative approach to young people's changing media environment in Europe'. *European Journal of Communication*, 13 (4), 435–56.

Livingstone, S. and Bovill, M. (eds) (2001) *Children and their Changing Media Environment: A European comparative study*. Mahwah, New Jersey and London: Lawrence Erlbaum Associates.

Mackay, H. (1997) *Generations: Baby boomers, their parents and their children*. Sydney: Macmillan.

Mannheim, K. (1952 [1928]) 'The problem of generations'. In K. Mannheim (ed), *Essays in the Sociology of Knowledge*. London: Routledge and Kegan Paul.

McNeal, J.U. (1992) *Kids as Customers: A handbook of marketing to children*. New York: Lexington Books.

Pasquier, D. (1996) 'Teen series' reception. Television, adolescence and culture of feelings'. *Childhood*, 3 (3), 351–73.

Qvortrup, J., Bardy, M., Sgritta, G. and Wintersberger, H. (eds) (1994) *Childhood Matters: Social theory, practice and politics*. Aldershot: Avebury.

Schulze, G. (1992) *Die Erlebnisgesellschaft: Kultursoziologie der Gegenwart*. Frankfurt and New York: Campus.

Sheldon, L. (1998) 'The middle years: children and television – cool or just plain boring?' In S. Howard (ed), *Young People and the Electronic Media*. London: UCL Press.

Stephens, S. (1997), 'Editorial introduction: children and nationalism'. *Childhood*, 1 (4), 5–18.

Werner, A. (1982) 'Geopolitisk sosalisering, miljobakgrunn og fjernsyn. En kryssnasjonal sammenlikning av barn i Norden'. *Tidssrift for samfunnsforskning*, 23, 207–30.

Weymann, A. (2000) 'Sozialer Wandel, Generationsverhältnisse und Technikgenerationen'. In M. Kohli and M. Szydlik (eds), *Generationen in Familien und Gesellschaft*. Opladen: Leske and Budrich.

6 Children, place, space and generation

Pia Christensen and Alan Prout

This chapter is concerned with relationships between children, place, space and generation. It uses material from one of the authors' ethnographic studies of children living in a village in Northern England and in Copenhagen in Denmark (Christensen 2003).[1] In this chapter we explore the relationship between place and space and relate this, in turn, to the perspectives of children and teachers. Through this we suggest that generation should be understood as both spatially and temporally constituted. Drawing on the ethnographic material, we show that the generational aspect of children's encounters with knowledges of space and place takes differing forms. In particular we show differing ways in which the distinction between space, as objectified general knowledge, and place, as local experiential knowledge, is handled by children and adults.

In an example based on fieldwork in England (see page 144), knowledge of space and place are socially and culturally constituted as separate. In this case the transmission of spatial ideas in the school setting displays generational practices that are more hierarchical than negotiative. Adults have little recognition of children's emplaced knowledge and this becomes subordinate to knowledge of space. Teachers explicate these practices through the use of spatial metaphors of direction that echo those used to constitute children's unaccompanied exploration of place as dangerous and in need of adult control.

However, in another example based on fieldwork in Denmark (see page 145), children's knowledge of space and place is interconnected. Their acquisition of spatial knowledge is connected to their collective

a locality, and this is accomplished in relationship
o recognise children's own emplaced understanding.
e also demonstrates that the problem of connecting
local kn.. :dge of place to spatial ideas is one shared by children
and adults.

Generation

We will begin, however, by discussing the recent re-emergence of
the concept of generation within the social study of childhood.
Although the term 'generation' has been employed within the
new social studies of childhood for over a decade, it is not until
recently that it has been the topic of more intense debate and
scrutiny (see, for example, Alanen 2001a). Within this discussion
differing notions of generation, with somewhat differing focuses of
attention, have emerged. In this chapter we will explore how each
of these approaches can illuminate our understanding of the
processes involved in children's creation of knowledge of space
and place.

A first distinction can be made between the anthropological and
sociological uses of the term. Traditionally, anthropologists have
been interested in generation as a component of kinship systems.
This has given rise to a large body of literature on kinship
classification, lineage and descent (for an introductory account to
these concepts see Parkin 1997; for a more contemporary perspective
see Carsten 2000). The sociological tradition, however, has centred
on two particular definitions, neither of which is especially concerned
with kinship: the conceptualisation of generation found in the
Mannheimian tradition, and more recent attempts within the
sociological study of childhood to rethink generation as a system
of relationships between adults and children.

The work of the German sociologist Karl Mannheim in the 1920s
continues as an active research tradition, especially in Germany, and
has also been influential internationally in the field of youth studies.

Its main focus is temporal. Embedded in a wider concern to explain social and cultural change, this formulation sees 'generations' as social units that come into existence when a cohort of people, born around the same time, grow up experiencing the same social and historical events and come to see themselves as a distinct generation group sharing common experience, values and attitudes. Mannheim explores the social factors that make this emergence possible but also suggests that once in existence, a 'generation' has an effect of its own on processes of social and cultural change. Mannheim draws a distinction between 'generation in itself' and 'generation for itself'. The former refers to the fact that a cohort was born into similar historical or social circumstances (the so-called 'generational location'). The latter refers to the possibility that the cohort members may come to think of and identify themselves as a distinct group. The main topics of empirical concern in this tradition are, therefore, the periodisation of birth circumstances (in terms of their social and historical particularities) and the discovery of whether, in fact, a given cohort does have a consciousness of itself as a distinct 'generation'. It should be noted that Mannheim sees 'youth', rather than childhood, as the key period for the formation of generation (see Chapter 2). This point gave rise to the influence of Mannheim on the sociology of youth in the post-war period, when 'youth subculture' rose to social prominence and awareness. However, many contemporary sociologists of childhood would suggest that childhood is also a period significant in the formation of generational consciousness.

The second sociological conception of generation, which we will call the 'structural approach', is much more recent. It has emerged from within the new social studies of childhood over the last decade (see Alanen 2001a). This approach seeks to establish the idea of a 'generational order' or system parallel to the notions of class order or gender order often employed by sociologists in speaking about social structure. In this definition, generation is seen as the system of relationships in which the positions of 'child' and that of 'adult' are produced. Alanen (2001a: 12) writes of generation that it can be thought of as:

> ... a socially constructed system of relationships among social positions in which children and adults are the holders of specific social positions defined in relation to each other and constituting in turn, specific (and in this case generational) structures.

In this respect the structural idea of generation is less explicitly concerned with change over time than is the Mannheimian one. It is more focused on the pattern of relationships between adults and children as they form a more or less enduring and stable feature of social systems.

The research questions prioritised by this approach are, therefore, concerned with '... detecting the both direct and indirect, invisible relations through which children are firmly embedded in structured sets of social relations that are larger than their very immediate local relations and potentially extending as far as the global social system' (Alanen 2001b: 142). This, it is argued, can be carried out by studies that examine the everyday lives of children in terms, *inter alia*, of practices of 'generationing', and by examining how the resources (material, social, and cultural) that particular practices of childhood depend upon become available.

In this chapter we do not wish to set these approaches against each other. Rather our discussion will focus on the experience and practice of generational relationships in specific settings. Through this we will show how each approach can contribute to understanding how children, space, place and generation become woven together.

Space and place

During the last two decades sociology, social geography and social theory have explored and elaborated the distinction between space and place. Although these terms are used in a multitude of different ways (see Crang and Thrift 2000), one theme that commonly emerges is 'space' as a way of delineating a three-dimensional physical environment in which objects and events occur and in which they have relative position and direction. 'Place', on the other hand, emerges as space invested with human meaning and significance. Auge (1995: 81–2), for example, speaks of place as 'symbolised' and space as the 'non-symbolised surfaces of the planet'.

This distinction has a notable history in sociological thinking. Goffman (1959), for example, was concerned with how settings convey cultural meaning and frame behaviour. 'Front stage' and 'back stage' emerge as more as 'places' than mere points in 'space'. Similarly, Giddens (1984: 182) adopts the term 'locales' to capture a similar sense of spaces being invested with meaningful interaction. However, a binary distinction between space and place is not ultimately sustainable because it implies the complete separation of nature and culture. Rather, following Latour (1991) we might say that 'space' and 'place' are both hybrids of nature and of culture. They are both created through a tangle of natural and social, human and non-human elements and processes. Attempts to make 'space' all natural delete the cultural and human work that goes into making it. Conversely, making 'place' all cultural deletes the elements of nature that necessarily go into the making of a place. This hybridity of and connection between space and place is what allows Merleau-Ponty to talk about narrative as the work that 'transforms places into spaces and spaces into places' (cited in Auge 1995: 80).

Ideas of space, then, arise in part from our interaction with the natural world and in part from sets of socially and historically located conventions for narrating or representing space. Anthropologists and geographers have, for example, drawn attention to the way in which people (including children: see Matthews 1992 and Christensen 2003) build cognitive maps of their environments. These are often very personal and idiosyncratic. Other forms of formal mapping, however, tend to have much more cultural visibility. Their aim is to represent space through a general knowledge intended to be used by many different people and for manifold purposes. These maps strip a place of its local particularities (and its social and personal content) and replace them with stylised symbols, stan-dardised classifications and disembedded, rational criteria, such as relative position, distance and scale. In doing so they *appear* to reflect spatial realities in an objective or neutral way – even though they actually (and inescapably) reflect a selective inclusion or exclusion of features of a landscape according to their purpose and the interests they serve (for example Conley 1996).

By representing highly generalised and abstract features of space, such as measurements of distance, such spatial inscriptions appear to be detached from local or particular social interests and mean-ings. In these circumstances a distinction between space and place, typical of post-Enlightenment thought, arises. As Casey puts it:

> Space is that about which we all must have *general* knowledge whereas we possess merely *local* knowledge about place.
>
> (Casey 1996: 16) (our emphasis)

Casey, then, contrasts spatial knowledge with an understanding of place. 'To live,' he writes, 'is to live locally and to know is first of all to know the places one is in' (Casey 1996: 18). Employing Merleau-Ponty's notions of an embodied phenomenology, he argues that human beings are always 'emplaced'. Both spaces and sensations are themselves emplaced from the very first moment and at every subse-quent moment as well. There is no knowing or sensing a place except by being in that place, moving around it and being in a position to perceive it.

In this sense the experience of place, he suggests, is not inferior to space; indeed, it can be seen as primary. However, formal, abstract and generalised knowledge of space is often performed as if it were superior to local knowledge. As a result of this, the separation between local knowledge of place and generalised knowledge of space is often implicated in conflicts over the uses to which particular spaces/places should be put. This is illustrated, for example, in conflicts between town planners and local people, which often involve a clash between planners' understanding of a space through its generalised properties, such as dimension and relative position, and local people's meanings of place and the significance that is invested in it. Opposition to the plans of developers is, in part, a product of the spatial perspective of the planners transgressing the emplaced meanings of local people.

Such place/space separation, however, also gives rise to another commonly experienced problem: how to reconnect knowledge of space with knowledge of place? Aligning spatial classifications with emplaced knowledge is often difficult. Reading a map, for example, is not a naturally given competence. It is something that has to be acquired or learned. Such learning consists of reconstituting a picture of how an actual, three-dimensional landscape may look from the symbolic two-dimensional representation of it on the map. Or it may be the other way around: learning to locate oneself in a space by reading the features of a landscape on to a map. A commonly shared experience of both adults and children is that this may indeed be a difficult task.

As these examples indicate, the connecting of spatial representations and emplaced knowledge is not only a problem for children. In this sense it is not in any essential way a 'generational' issue. However, it clearly is a problem that has a definite salience for children, as we will go on to show. Their integration into a society and a culture requires that they actively grapple with both the concrete specifics of their local places and the general representational codes that are used in relation to describing and representing space. This is especially true in complex societies, which depend in many ways on a shared understanding of spatial representations. In such circumstances possessing spatial knowledge becomes an important form of cultural capital.

Children's emplaced knowledge

Before returning to the distinction between space and place, we will discuss some of the ways in which children develop their knowledge of place. Drawing on her fieldwork in Northern England and Copenhagen, Christensen has recently (2003) shown some of the ways that children encounter places, construct and perceive them, and invest them with significance. During their lifecourse, she argues, children are engaged in constructing and understanding their personal biography in and of particular spatial localities. Using both participant observation and interviews with children, she shows how these children map their experiences and memories of growing up on to spaces. As these come into place so, at the same time, the children themselves come into place. She demonstrates how children's understandings of themselves are developed through their experiences, memories and use of their houses, streets, villages, neighbourhoods, and their cities at large. In her study, children related their experiences and memories of growing up to their changing mobility in and between their houses, neighbourhoods and their wider environment (whether village, town or city). Their changing mobility in and between these different spaces and their bodily experience of them was important to how they saw themselves achieving independence, competence and maturity and to how they formed and sustained their social relations with peers.

In mapping their personal biographies, children engaged with place as a simultaneously social and physical location, describing how they came to inhabit and belong to a place through their experiences and uses of it. For example, in the following extract from Christensen's fieldwork diary, a ten-year-old boy, Bill, remembered his earlier childhood in terms of a particular tree:

At the corner of the street where Bill lives he suddenly stops and points to a tree: 'My little tree!' he exclaims. I ask him whether this is the tree he used to climb and Bill explains: 'We used to climb when we

were little ... we used to play in the tree behind my house – you know,
where the patio is now, when we were little, it was there ... Yeah, it
was only small though, only about this big (he shows us in the air how
small it had been) ... but it got a lot, it's bigger now.'

Conversations with the children also revealed the way in which a sense
of place was sometimes woven together with that of kinship. Some
children emphasised their connection to the village through seeing
themselves as continuing to live within the local area when they grew
up and had their own families. This sense of belonging locally was
most strongly revealed in the farming families, where family members
were tied to the farm and the land through the family extending across
the generations. In youth and throughout their adult life these families
lived in the farmhouse, having the main responsibility for the land.
Eventually the older generation would retire into a bungalow or one
of the cottages in the village, where other kin sometimes lived. For
example, one boy's grandmother was soon going to move to a house
on a newly built estate. Standing in front of the bungalow where she
would live, he immediately identified it as such and, pointing to the
bare soil in the garden, explained that, 'I rotivated it up ... Look the
house (next door) is sold and that's our plough.' Thus the spatial
distribution of land and patterns of residence within the villages offer a
graphic representation of the interconnectedness of family, kin and
generation.

An important part of the children's accounts concerns the way in
which children shared experiences of place. This does not mean that
all children had the same experiences or that they inscribed the same
meanings on to particular spaces or read the same meanings from
them. Sometimes the children would contest between themselves the
significance of a place. This emerged, for example, in a walk that
Christensen conducted with a group of children around one of
the villages. The local life of the ducks in the village pond gave rise
not only to a discussion of the constitution of duck families through
the birth and upbringing of the little ducklings but also to a discussion

among the children about who really 'belonged' to the village and who did not. This is recorded in a fieldwork note:

> Before we leave Rebecca and Tom tell us that one of the swans living on the pond was shot with an air catapult. This was a story reported in the local newspaper, the *Woldsby Tatler*, where they had both read about it. Rebecca holds her leg up towards the remaining swan urging it to come closer to us: 'Eat my shoe, swan, I want some more (shoes).' This talk about the *Woldsby Tatler* brings on a discussion among the children. They are concerned whether Tom, who lives in a country house outside the village, actually belongs in Woldsby when he does not receive the *Tatler* through the post. Tom thinks they ought to have one sent because he still lives in Woldsby, although his house is out in the country. Bill and Rebecca think he does not belong to the village because he does not receive the paper. Tom insists that his house is in Woldsby Parish. Rebecca tells us that her parents have to go to another village to vote for the election – but they still belong to Woldsby.

However, this very discussion underlines the point that in large part the meaning of place was not just an individual one for children. The children were engaged in collectively exploring the village through not only the material but also the social and cultural world they lived in. The children discussed and established its inhabitants, their status and their social, material and kin relations in order to work out the significance of their local places. Sometimes they would do this as a group, sharing common experiences. Or they would discuss the meaning of a particular place from their differing personal experiences and come to a shared understanding of it. In this sense the children can be seen as a cohort growing up together and sharing common understandings as they do so. As noted above, in Mannheim's conception of generation this common experience of a cohort passing through time together is a necessary but not sufficient condition for the formation of a generational unit. Mannheim assumes these processes to take place during 'youth' but, as these examples suggest, these processes can be seen to start in childhood. Furthermore, the examples underline the point that such a formation of a possible 'generation' involves not only a common temporal framework but also that place (and its apprehension and construction) is implicated in the process. Common meanings are attached to places as well as historical events, experiences and periods.

Generationing knowledge of space and place

Having suggested that children's exploration of their local environment is important in developing their sense of themselves and of place, we can now turn to the relationship of these to knowledge of space. As we noted above, there is often a mismatch between emplaced knowledge and the abstract and formal knowledge of space, such as that found in maps, which requires some work of reconnection. We also noted that in modern societies children are required to develop a general knowledge of space. But how do they do this? In the next section we will discuss two contrasting practices of connection as they appeared in the fieldwork. These show that space and place can be aligned in differing ways. We suggest that the differences between these examples point to the way in which different assemblies of generation intersect with the problem of space and place.

The examples are drawn from studies conducted in England and Denmark. In the first example, drawn from an English school, we will illustrate how the generational relationships enacted around space and place draw on a hierarchical model. Teachers were essentially concerned with transmitting knowledge of space in its formal, generalised aspect. They paid relatively little attention to children's own practices and experiences of place. In this sense they treated knowledge of place and space as separate. The children were required to absorb spatial ideas more or less independently of their experience of bodily sensing and movement through a locality. This, however, can be contrasted with examples from Denmark, where the sets of relationships between children, teachers and pedagogues regarding place might be seen to form a more negotiative practice. The teachers and pedagogues connected children's emplaced knowledge with that of formalised space, drawing on their senses, social meanings and their bodily experiences of place.

The English school that Christensen studied was a small village school in the north of England with only 56 children, who were separated in two non-age-segregated classes. The example concerns one of these classes – the seven- to 11-year-olds and their teacher. For a couple of weeks during the spring term their geography lessons were dedicated to learning about their local area. The lessons centred on the regional capital, Sealford, a large coastal town about 20 miles from where they lived. The teacher planned to conclude the project with a one-day school trip to visit and look around the town and beach. The children were asked to draw maps locating the town and pencilling in its size and shape. Most lessons, however, were dedicated to engaging the children with the knowledge that can be drawn out about a place from using the telephone directory. Through developing their skills in using the index pages and working their way around the various sections of the many-paged book, the children were to learn about the place they lived in.

For most children this was a rather tedious job. Although they were able to choose whether they wanted to work alone or in pairs, it was often a slow process. The children's task was to make lists of, for example, how many primary schools, how many doctors, dentists and other local services and institutions there were in the area. The children were required not only to list the different services in numbers but also to check that the area code of the telephone number was correct and that the address was indeed located in Sealford. They then had to copy the names of the doctors or dentists on to their paper. There was not much scope for children's own ideas and interests when conducting this task. The most fun the children had with this task was to giggle about 'what silly names doctors had' or break out in surprise at the number of primary schools in Sealford.

In the Danish school, the learning context for space and place was different in approach. It drew on the idea of teaching children about local physical spaces and local geography in a quite literal sense, through the body. In a physical education lesson, the fourth graders were asked to take a tour around their local area. The children were provided with a sheet of paper listing a range of particular spots together with a map showing an enlarged section of the local area. The task of the children was to find their way around the local neighbourhood, locating particular spots using the road name and house number given on the paper.

The questions on the sheet were, for example: 'What colour is the gate of number 26 on Maple Street (Ahornvej)?' or 'What are the colours of the window frames of number 17 Oak Street (Egeskov-vej)?' The questionnaire created a circular walk taking the children around a particular part of their local neighbourhood and through the streets surrounding the school. On the way the children walked, ran, jumped up in the air, kicked stones and engaged in discussing what they saw. For example, suddenly finding themselves in front of a friend's house, they responded with, 'That's where Emma lives!' and, 'That's Martin's house!' A barking dog made some children scared and they passed it by walking in a big circle and cautiously keeping a safe distance. Others stopped and for a little while discussed whether to appease the dog, estimating the danger they would face if it suddenly ran loose. The trip was set up almost as a game. The children explored the local area through active movement and using their senses. As one eleven-year-old girl later described it:

It was because we were to use our muscles and our brains.

The children used their skills, such as sense of direction and local knowledge, to read the map – sometimes figuring out what would be the best shortcuts on the route. They observed colours, cracks in walls, bent road signs, flowers and guessed missing house numbers, all details that sometimes had gone unnoticed on earlier visits, and they came to explore places they had not been before. They had new experiences and they related these to earlier experiences or to the experiences of other children.

One after-school club in the same area also took up the theme of achieving local knowledge for children. As the children attending the club came from various local areas, the clubs arranged a number of trips to allow the children to explore the city. While some of the children lived in the neighbourhood of the school and after-school club, other children lived outside the local area. In the club's monthly diary these trips appeared as: 'We will go round to see where we all live.' Every Wednesday afternoon for two months in late spring a group of children went to visit the house of one of the other children. Central to this experience was the excitement of doing these trips together. 'Everybody is going!' the children proclaimed, and the visit to the houses was seen as a treat: 'We are going to Rikke's house and we will play and perhaps have soft drinks.' During most visits the children would in fact spend time playing outside and then have a snack or make a picnic before they set off back to the club.

The changing context of schooling

The point of these contrasting examples described above is not that generational relationships in Danish schools are *necessarily* more negotiative than ones in the UK. Schools differ, and no doubt counter-examples from both Denmark and England could be found. Perhaps, too, generational relations in a school are not necessarily stable or consistent. A particular school, for example, might change from hierarchical to negotiative orderings and vice versa. Various teachers (or parents and children) in the same school may also have differing practices with regard to the relationship between children and adults or between the curriculum and children's experience. Similarly children may experience a different relationship with adults at home compared with school. Rather, the examples illustrate two different practices for handling the relationship between knowledge of space and place. Both the hierarchical and the negotiative instances of these can be seen as addressing the issue of how to connect different modes of knowledge, but they have different implications for generational relationships.

It is notable, therefore, that Christensen's interviews with teachers in the English school suggest that they were well aware that their relationship with the children – and the disconnection between what children learnt at school and their everyday experience – could have been otherwise. They too felt constrained by a set of changes that had been imposed upon them by national education policy. The example of school activities not connecting very well with children's emplaced knowledge is, in fact, an instance of a wider question in discussions of the current context of children's learning experiences in England. The introduction of a national curriculum, a system of national learning standards, and the periodic testing of children against these has meant that time has become a scarce resource in English schools (Christensen and James 2001). The teachers suggested that there is little time to connect with children's own experiences and explorations. The imbalance thus created between the different aspects of learning has led to concerns about the conditions and prospects for children's imaginative and creative abilities and their broad cultural development (Pollard *et al.* 1994; Pollard 1996; Almond 1999; Carvel 1999). The consequence for children is that they feel they lack control over how they spend their time at school (Christensen and James 2001). This has detrimental effects on children's experiences of their schooling and makes it more difficult for the school to have a meaningful place in their everyday lives and their personal life project.

The teachers experienced the national curriculum as having serious disadvantages affecting their teaching and in their relationship to the children. As one teacher saw it, primary education was ideally about creating opportunities for children through an early exposure to a wealth of different experiences:

Just *opening up avenues* for them for later life, involvement in as many
things as possible that they may then pick up at secondary school and
clubs at the weekends ... I have pupils who come back to me after
years, who've said, 'Thanks for introducing me to table tennis because
I've gone and enjoyed that activity over the years.'

(our emphasis)

However, while stressing that in his view this was a 'very, very
important aspect of primary education', this teacher acknowledged
that this broader educational goal was now increasingly at risk.
What he described as 'the press of standards, standards, standards'
was making it necessary for schools to give priority to reaching
the educational targets set out for them within the framework of
the national curriculum rather than engaging with children's
experiences.

In another teacher's view, the emphasis on testing and standards
has meant that 'you are increasingly teaching more and more and
more for children to jump through narrow hoops'. She saw this
emphasis on standards and testing as leading to deterioration in
child–adult relations at school:

> ... the rapport in schools sometimes goes down because teachers
> perpetually feel under pressure to perform to these results and that has
> an effect on the way that they conduct their lessons ... there isn't scope
> any more for sort of saying, 'That's a great point! Let's investigate
> that,' picking up things that the children initiate and actually *running
> with them.*
>
> (our emphasis)

As a consequence of these pressures, then, the project of schooling has
become increasingly in the teachers', rather than the child's, power
and under their authority. One headteacher described the process:

> You'll start a lesson and you'll find that the children's interest is
> leading you towards a certain path and it's not in your plan. In the

past you'd have *gone down that path* because the children were interested. Nowadays you're very much a case of, 'This isn't in my plan and I didn't intend this to happen, stop it and let's *get back on track.*'

(our emphasis)

Children in school and children in place

It is noticeable that in the teachers' accounts related above there is frequent use of spatial metaphors to describe the processes of teaching and learning and the effects of these on the national curriculum. These include 'opening avenues', 'jumping through hoops', 'running', 'paths', and 'getting back on track'. The sense conveyed by these is that in the regime of the national curriculum children's own explorations and senses posed the threat of leading them astray and that teachers were required to take the lead, keep control and show direction.

There is a striking parallel here between the metaphors of teaching and learning employed by these teachers and the danger that children's mobility and independent exploration of their local area is often seen to pose. As Lakoff and Turner (1989: 3) point out, metaphors of destination are often used to express the idea of a purpose or goal:

When we think of life as purposeful, we think of it as having destinations and paths towards those destinations ...

The educational changes described above were intended to strengthen this idea: that English children's experiences of schools should be of pre-defined destinations. The changes were intended to displace a set of practices that had allowed children to learn at their own pace through 'exploration', a process that was being understood as a relatively directionless 'wander' through experiences, ideas and information. In the 1980s these practices became the target of a wide-ranging political attack, blamed for everything from supposedly falling educational standards to economic failure and moral decay. Political parties of all colours became committed to 'raising standards' through reforms that were seen as putting more discipline and structure into schooling. These took the form of directions, signposts and milestones, and teachers were seen as responsible for ensuring that children followed and met them.

In this context public discussion of children increasingly took place through discourses emphasising children as 'the future'. Prout (2000) has suggested that during this period children were constituted as one of the few remaining ways of controlling the future in a world seen as increasingly uncertain and resistant to established forms of control such as economic management and scientific rationality.

Modern societies have long been marked by their concern to keep children in their 'proper place' – usually at home or in school and away from the street or other public space (Lee 2001: 55–86). At the same time that children's space was being subjected to more regulation and control so too was there an intensification of concern about children in public space. Children's wandering the street was seen as increasingly dangerous (either to them as victims of crime or traffic or because they would victimise others). In Matthews *et al.*'s (2000) memorable phrase, children became 'the unacceptable flaneur', not only in their wanderings through space and place but also in learning.

Conclusions

In this chapter we have explored some of the ways in which generation, place and space are connected. From this discussion we can, first, note that none of the three available concepts of generation (the kinship, the Mannheimian or the structural) is adequate on its own. Each, however, should be respected for the partial picture it helps to bring into focus and reveal. Generation in its kinship aspect, for example, is important to children because their relations with people are part of the way they read places and form a sense of attachment with them. Some children, as we have seen, belong to a place because it is where their relatives lived, and they too sense that they belong to it for this reason.

The Mannheimian concept is concerned with the passage of time and the emergence of generation groups who identify themselves and recognise others in terms of their common experiences as a cohort. In this chapter we have suggested that common experiences are located not only in time but also in space and place. We have also suggested that the formation of common experience, embedded in place, starts in childhood and is not necessarily postponed until later youth. Another way of saying this is that a lifecourse perspective on 'growing up' remains important to the study of childhood. Consequently any notion of generation that downplays this is in danger of missing an important aspect of childhood experience.

The structural concept of childhood is helpful too. It draws attention to the relationships between adults and children and the way these are produced. In particular, it is useful in drawing attention to the way generational relationships in a particular milieu are shaped by more widespread influences. The effect of the national curriculum on the English school described above illustrates this point. At the same time, however, our comparison of two schools suggests that generational ordering is plural, not unitary. In this paper, two rather different 'orderings' of generation can be seen. In this case these were distributed in different schools in different countries, but further work may find different orderings jostling alongside each other in settings closer to each other. It is, we suggest, best to leave open to empirical investigation how different practices of generation are distributed between and across contexts. We may have, then, to think not of a single generational order from which instances can be read off but rather of partial generational orderings. These may have relative stability, but they are also in process and can prove fragile. Different orderings can remain apart from each other but they also come into contact, interact, overlap or clash with each other.

The structural concept of generation should be treated as a partial account in another sense: it is one that seems to privilege inter-generational relationships. Left to its own logic, it runs the risk of neglecting intra-generational relationships, those between children themselves, in what are often called their peer cultures and or peer relationships. In this chapter we have suggested that the collective practices of children themselves are important in constructing their sense of place. In part, children engage with a locality collectively. They make their own meanings about these localities through their own practices and discussions. Their practices may make new meanings, different from those of older generations and specific to children's own emplaced knowledge that is also situated in time.

Many, if not most, adults also depend in their everyday lives on emplaced knowledge of localities. The children and adults who coinhabit a locality are likely to share a great deal of emplaced knowledge, even while the children are engaged in contributing their own generational content. Furthermore, many disparities between spatial and emplaced knowledge do not take only a generational form. However, the relationship between spatial and emplaced knowledge can be *given* a generational aspect. This happens, for example, when knowledge of space is required as part of a person's cultural capital. This is often a requirement of modern societies and is one that has been intensified and brought under surveillance by the recent changes in educational policy. For parents and teachers it is an important task to equip children with such cultural capital, even if it does not connect very well with local, meaningful, emplaced knowledge. In this sense the adults and children in both settings discussed in this paper seem to be addressing the same problem, but in differing ways. In this chapter we have suggested how the distinction between place and space can both contribute to and draw on different ways of constructing generational relationships.

Note

1   The UK study, the Changing Times project, was carried out with Allison James and Chris Jenks. It involved ten-year-old children living in two villages and a provincial city in the north of England. The study was funded by the ESRC as

part of the Children 5–16 Research Programme (Award L129 25 1025). The Danish data derive from a study about children's time, *Born og Tid*, that Pia Christensen carried out with children and young people living in a local district of Copenhagen. This study was funded by the Danish Research Council's research programme Children's Living Conditions and Welfare. We wish to thank both funding bodies for providing financial support for the research and are grateful to all the children and young people who participated in the studies.

References

Alanen, L. (2001a) 'Explorations in generational analysis'. In L. Alanen and B. Mayall (eds), *Conceptualising Child-Adult Relations*. London: RoutledgeFalmer.

— (2001b) 'Childhood as a generational condition: children's daily lives in a central Finland town'. In L. Alanen and B. Mayall (eds), *Conceptualising Child-Adult Relations*. London: RoutledgeFalmer.

Almond, D. (1999) *Leave Time for Imagination*. London: The Independent, 15 July.

Auge, M. (1995) *Non-Places: An introduction to an anthropology of supermodernity*. London: Verso.

Carsten, J. (ed) (2000) *Cultures of Relatedness: New approaches to the study of kinship*. Cambridge: Cambridge University Press.

Carvel, J. (1999) *A Vision Under the Microscope*. London: The Guardian, 2 November.

Casey, E. (1996) 'How to get from space to place in a fairly short stretch of time: phenomenological prolegomena'. In S. Feld and K. Basso (eds), *Senses of Place*. Santa Fe: SAR Press.

Christensen, P. (2003) 'Place, space and knowledge: children in the village and the city'. In P. Christensen and M. O'Brien (eds), *Children and the City*. London: RoutledgeFalmer.

Christensen, P. and James, A. (2001) 'What are schools for? The temporal experience of schooling.' In L. Alanen and B. Mayall (eds), *Conceptualising Child-Adult Relations*. London: RoutledgeFalmer.

Conley, T. (1996) *The Self-Made Map: Cartographic writing in early modern France*. Minneapolis: University of Minnesota Press.

Crang, M. and Thrift, N. (eds) (2000) *Thinking Space*. London: Routledge.

Giddens, A. (1984) *The Constitution of Society*. Cambridge: Polity Press.

Goffman, E. (1959) *The Presentation of Self in Everyday Life*. Harmondsworth: Penguin.

Lakoff, G. and Turner, M. (1989) *More than Cool Reason: A field guide to poetic metaphor*. Chicago: Chicago University Press.

Latour, B. (1991) *We Have Never Been Modern.* Hemel Hempstead: Harvester Wheatsheaf.

Lee, N. (2001) *Children and Society: Growing up in an age of uncertainty.* Buckingham: Open University Press.

Matthews, H. (1992) *Making Sense of Place: Children's understanding of large-scale environments.* Hemel Hempstead: Harvester Wheatsheaf.

Matthews, H., Taylor, M., Percy-Smith, B. and Limb, M. (2000) 'The unacceptable *flaneur*: the shopping mall as a teenage hangout'. *Childhood,* 7 (3), 279–94.

Parkin, R. (1997) *Kinship: An introduction to the basic concepts.* Oxford: Blackwell.

Pollard, A. (1996) *The Social World of Children's Learning.* London: Cassell.

Pollard, A., Broadfoot, P., Croll, P. and Abbot, D. (1994) *Changing English Primary Schools.* London: Cassell.

Prout, A. (2000) *Children's participation: control and self-realisation in British late modernity.* Special Millennium Edition of *Children and Society,* 14 (4), 304–15.

Part Four
Historical dynamics in the
development of childhood

7 Intergenerational relations and social change in childhood: examples from West Germany

Helga Zeiher

Translated from the German by Susannah Goss

Two conceptualisations of 'generation' and their interconnections

Twenty years ago, a book entitled *War Children, Consumer Children, Crisis Children: On the history of socialisation since the Second World War* was published in Germany (Preuss-Lausitz *et al.* 1983). A working group of West German sociologists, all of whom had been born around 1940 and were aged about 40 at the time, had gathered together in 1980 with the aim of jointly addressing our 'irritation at the behaviour of today's children and adolescents', as we later wrote in the preface to our book. We felt that we as a generation had lived a very different childhood from that experienced by our juniors, and hoped that, by examining the differences between these childhoods in more detail, we would gain a deeper understanding of our own relationships to the children of the day. What were the implications of the initial post-war period, and subsequently of the German 'economic miracle' and the upheavals of the late 1960s, for the childhoods and the biographies of those growing up at the time? Which particular experiences shaped each generation of children? Could the difficulties that the various post-war generations had with one another be traced back to these different childhood experiences?

These questions led to a comparative study of successive childhood generations, the approach based on the theory formulated by Karl

Mannheim (1952 [1928]) (see Chapter 2). Mannheim defined generations as groups of people born into the world at approximately the same time, who are 'endowed ... with a common location in the historical dimension of the social process' of a particular society by the time of their birth (ibid: 290). They form a 'generation as actuality' when linked by their 'participation in the common destiny', and become a 'generational unit' when processing their experiences in the same way (ibid: 303). He suggested that the ways in which experiences are processed are determined by the point of the 'stratification of experience' in the individual lifecourse; that is, the point in the lifecourse at which the experiences occur. Mannheim emphasised the 'predominance of early impressions'.

> ... it is important to know whether it is undergone by an individual as a decisive childhood experience, or later in life, superimposed upon basic and early impressions. Early impressions tend to coalesce into a *natural view* of the world. All later experiences then tend to receive their meaning from this original set, whether they appear as that set's verification and fulfilment or as its negation and antithesis.
>
> (ibid: 298)

Whereas Mannheim – like other authors who have studied the formation of historical generations – focused on youth, our working group started earlier in the lifecourse, namely in childhood. The group aimed at combining two approaches to the study of childhood that had come to the fore in West Germany in the 1970s – socialisation theory and research on the history of childhood. Our attention was directed to conditions that at the time had been established as the 'hidden curriculum' of the everyday world, which was crucial in the process of socialisation, namely the concrete opportunities and constraints for children's daily lives that were inherent in the spatial, temporal, material and cultural realities of the everyday world. We studied the ways in which children responded to these conditions and interacted with adults. Historical childhoods were distinguished from one another, each being described as a set of circumstances in which the social world of adults shaped children's daily lives in a historically particular way, and which was characterised by particular relationships between children and adults. By looking concretely at particular historical childhoods, we gave less prominence to questions about a possible later socialisation output and instead focused on children's daily activities and interrelations. Thus we regarded childhood as a socially constructed relationship maintained between children and adults in their roles as people of different ages living side by side. This conceptualisation corresponds to later ideas from sociologists of childhood (see Chapter 1).

The 1980 working group implicitly considered relations between a diachronic and a synchronic conceptualisation of 'generation' in their work: a historical approach following Mannheim's concept of a succession of particular youth generation groups[1] – different birth cohorts – in the course of time, and an approach focusing on the social relations between the younger and older generations, the children and the adults, living at the same time. Now, twenty years later, both approaches to the generation issue enjoy great popularity in Germany, but they define distinct realms of research. In the social sciences, research into the biographical effects of life under National Socialism, in particular, has revived academic interest in the formation of historical generations and the relations between them, not only from the historiographical but also from the theoretical perspective (for example Rosenthal 1997; Bude 2000). In the 1990s both family sociologists (Lüscher and Schultheis 1993; Mansel *et al.* 1997) and educational scientists (such as Liebau and Wulf 1996; Ecarius 1998) have studied generational relationships. Newspaper feature writers often think up new labels for cohort generations, seeking to persuade their readers that today's young people act in ways that are new and different (cf. Uhle 1996).

On the other hand, relations between adults and children are conceptualised and examined as generational relations in the sociology of childhood. Although research in this field in Germany has continued to focus on recent social change, little attention has been paid to successive generation groups and to the way in which their confrontation might contribute to an explanation of present-day childhood. This aspect has been addressed only in the eastern part of Germany, where the social upheavals following the collapse of the GDR regime prompted researchers to compare childhoods before and after German reunification, and to explore the extent to which a new childhood generation group was being formed (Kirchhöfer 1998). Apart from this, however, German research on the sociology of childhood has described tendencies in social change without considering successive generation groups or the relationships between them.

The time may now have come to recombine the two conceptualisations of 'generation'. In this chapter, I would like to show that this may help us to gain a deeper understanding of the present-day relations between adults and children and of current developments in the generational order of society. Then, in a historiographical perspective, I will suggest that social change may be considered not only in terms of historic tendencies, but also as a succession of generation groups, each characterised by particular experiences of relations between adults and children in their childhood. In such a perspective, the historically specific adult-child relations can be regarded as relations between historically differently 'located' generation groups. As members of a certain generation group, adults interact with children in particular ways, and this may produce a dynamic that contributes to shape the particularity of these children's childhoods. It may even trigger the genesis of a new generation group of children.

I should like to consider in more detail two forms of interconnection between children and adults, since both involve intergenerational dynamics. These are based on two simple facts which ensure that children cannot avoid interacting with adults: children do not spend all of their time with their peers, but also in the company of adults; and children are dependent on adults, most directly on their parents.

Firstly, children and adults represent people of differing ages with differing biographical experiences. It is not only on account of the social position related to their age group, but also because of the specific 'stratification of experience' of their generation group, that children and adults are affected differently by current events, and that they perceive and respond to occurrences in different ways. Because children spend much of their time with adults, much of what they experience is based partly or exclusively on the way in which adults are affected by events. Elder and Caspi have described this kind of interdependence in the lifecourses of those belonging to different age groups: 'In the lives of individuals, social change is expressed through the experiences of others; "macro"-events impact on individual development through the dynamics of interdependent life courses' (1991: 45). The authors emphasise this interdependence as being of particular relevance in the context of the family, where children's everyday lives are profoundly affected by the ways in which historical events impact on their parents' lives. In his well-known study *Children of the Great Depression*, Elder (1974) showed how the dramatic losses of earnings their parents suffered in the world economic crisis changed the everyday lives of North American children at the beginning of the 1930s.

Secondly, children are dependent on adults. This is due to the anthropological fact that humans continue to develop after birth. Children are born in need of help, and for years – though to an ever-lessening extent – they are dependent on the protection and care of adults, and on adults integrating them into society. In all societies, this is transformed and constructed as a generational relation, a generational order of childhood and adulthood, and is expressed in the definitions and structures of childhood. The generational order of every society represents a particular societal form of the anthropological difference and dependency, and thus involves control as well as integration/segregation. In their respective positions in the generational order of a society, adults and children meet as members of different historically located generation groups. Interactions between adults and children are influenced not only by patterns of the generational order of the current society, but also by the specific take on these which is based on personal biographies. In daily life, this can lead to disputes and conflicts between children and adults. On the socio-structural level, it can lead to dynamics that impact on the future development of the generational order of society. This may be the case, for example, when the members of a generation group enter adulthood and, in the light of their own childhood experiences, seek to interact with children in an entirely different way, and to create conditions very different from those that characterised their own childhood.

Previous experiences are not directly relevant in such interactions and responses. Rather, it is a question of how biographical 'stratifications of experiences' are activated in given situations, how they are confronted with the reality of the present day, and how they are subject to constant reorganisation and reinterpretation (see, for example, Rosenthal 1997; Bude 2000). In this chapter, such processes will not be considered. Instead, the focus is on the formation of historically distinct childhoods. As stated above, this implies historical differences in the levels of control and integration characterising the relations between the generation groups who are at a time interacting as children and adults. I am particularly interested in the generation groups' specific 'themes' originating in the everyday lives of children, especially in their interactions with their parents.

I will pursue this interest by examining a particular succession of childhood generation groups in West Germany. First, I will portray those who were children during the Second World War, referring to the description the members of the working group gave in their book. I will then address the question that the research group failed to answer at that time, and consider the next generation – the war children's children. Finally, I will go one step further and consider the children of the present day.

The generation group of war children

We, as members of the working group, compiled memories of our own childhoods in the war and early post-war years and conducted oral history interviews with our peers. In which respects had the economic, political and cultural conditions prevailing at and immediately after the end of the war affected children's everyday lives? Again and again, the reports referred to playing outside. Because living space was urgently required for those who had lost their homes in the bombing and for refugees from the Eastern territories, there was very little room left for children to play in the flats. Instead, they played outside as much as possible. In retrospect, the bombed-out ruins had been wonderful playgrounds, full of dangers. Like the improvised ways of making a living – from collecting wood and stealing apples to black marketeering – they were seen as a great adventure. The children were mainly free from adult supervision when playing outside. Even at home, adults did not exert a great deal of influence since, at this point, only a few fathers had returned home from the front or from captivity, and the mothers were busy taking care of the bare necessities. In other words, these children enjoyed a high degree of freedom in the initial post-war period; however, it seemed clear that this was not due to any change in their parents' attitudes to child-rearing following the defeat of the National Socialist regime, but to the simple fact that adults had very little time for them.

Because no such change in adults' attitudes occurred, the new-found freedom was soon lost, and the habitual order of the family and society was restored in the 1950s. Fathers returning home reasserted their authority; mothers reverted to subordinate roles as housewives. Thus, during the war children's childhood, the controls had been relaxed for a short period, only to be tightened again shortly afterwards. We described this as a historical control gap.

The experience of liberty in early childhood and restriction in later childhood and youth, the clash between the absence of control and its subsequent restoration formed the war children born after 1939 into a 'generation as actuality' (Mannheim) that was particularly well motivated and qualified to rebel against suppression and authoritarian traditions. The birth cohort 1939 marked a clear boundary here. Although those born only slightly earlier, in the mid-1930s, had also experienced the control gap, they had also been consciously aware of threat and deprivation during and immediately after the war. Consequently, these older cohorts associated freedom from control with fear and insecurity. Only the younger cohorts were free from these concerns; only they were in a position to repeat the upheavals they had experienced in childhood by breaking down the restorative and authoritarian societal structures in their adolescent years. Indeed, 'generational units' (Mannheim) of those born after 1939 produced both the hooligan rebellions of the late 1950s and the student movement of the 1960s. As young adults at the end of the 1960s, they demanded radical change in intergenerational power relations, and actually succeeded in effecting such change in the context of the economic transformation to a service society that was taking place at the time. As educational policy makers and educationalists, members of this generation effected the structural reform of the educational system. As developmental psychologists and socialisation theorists, they formulated a new conception of the child as a self-determined subject responsible for his or her own socialisation, while a broad middle class of parents, carers and teachers deemed independence to be the most important objective of child-rearing (Preuss-Lausitz *et al.* 1990).

As social scientists, our research questions and criteria were based on a critical appraisal of our own childhood experiences. We aimed to find a way of ensuring the dehierarchisation of relations between adults and children. Children were to be taken seriously, both in their personal relationships to their parents and teachers and in their responses to the structural realities of their daily lives. In order to find out whether we succeeded in effecting this change, we studied the personal relationships between parents and children and explored how structural change in daily life affected children's opportunities for self-determined agency (du Bois-Reymond *et al.* 1994; Zeiher and Zeiher 1994). The members of the 1980 working group ourselves belonged to this group of social scientists from the war-children generation group. In conclusion, it can be stated that our generation group was characterised by a particular sensitivity to power relations, and that its dominant 'theme' was the breakdown of patriarchal authority and social control.

The war children's children – a new childhood generation group?

At the time our book was published, the members of the working group had not arrived at identifying 'what kind of a childhood generation [was] growing up', and childhood researchers of the later 1980s were no more successful. Although the title of the book referred not only to 'war children', but to 'consumer children' and 'crisis children', the first part of the book attempted to characterise as a whole only the generation group of those born around 1960. In the second part of the book, entitled 'Childhood Today: Changes and Upheavals', changes in the everyday lives and conditions of those born since the mid-1960s – the war children's children – were described, but no picture of a new generation group emerged. In other words, the question that we set out to address remained unanswered. Had no new childhood generation group been formed, or had we failed to identify it as such?

The end of the war and National Socialism had been a pivotal moment in the lives of most of those who experienced it, one that drastically changed the everyday living conditions of almost all families and the lives of the children in them. Over the following decades ways of life changed radically, too, but this was a gradual process, touching different sections of the population at different times and to different degrees. There were, however, turning points in this process of change, points at which long-term processes intensified, accelerated and climaxed. A radical upheaval occurred in the mid-1960s, when the affluent society grew rapidly, the service sector expanded, the information media gained in importance, the educational system was reformed, and new cultural patterns became predominant. This accumulation of changes in various domains of everyday life also implied a 'push of modernisation' for childhood. The project of modernity, which was to effect the social differentiation of childhood from adulthood as a structural context and social status, and to make childhood into a special protective and preparatory sphere, made great progress during this period. The reform of the educational system meant that all children spent a larger proportion of their time in institutions specifically geared to their needs – schools, preschool childcare, and recreation facilities. Those working in the expanding fields of the educational and developmental sciences came to perceive all children's actions – including playing – as learning, and rationalised and normalised this. From this point on, the everyday life of children was increasingly characterised by formal organisation, the efficient use of time, segregation in child-specific places, and learning performance expectations. Increases in traffic led to children staying more inside playgrounds and houses, too (cf Zeiher 2001a).

In order to find out whether and in what way these changes in childhood structures led to the formation of a new generation group, we sought to identify phenomena in the children's ways of living and acting. We were guided by our interest in questions of control, the theme dominating our own generation. We drew attention to changes in dependencies and forms of control in children's everyday lives that had accompanied the rapid modernisation. It turned out that, by now, inter-generational power relations had assumed a new, contradictory character. On the one hand, children's activities were more closely bound to specialised structures; on the other hand, children were now in more of a position to decide which of the available options they wished to pursue. On the one hand, the differentiated structures and concepts implied a high degree of structural control, thus including children in the transformation from personal to structural control that had been taking place in the world of work. On the other hand, adults endeavoured to establish egalitarian, rather than authoritarian, relationships with children. Research projects at the time diagnosed a tendency towards dehierarchisation and informalisation of the personal interactions between children and their parents, a shift 'from giving and obeying orders to negotiating' (Büchner 1983). We, in common with other social scientists of the time, discussed these contradictions in the conditions of childhood, advocated children's agency and self-determination, and registered any autonomous activity that diverged from the set structures with particular approval (for example, when children did not confine themselves to playgrounds or restrict their activities to those intended by playground designers). But how had the children themselves responded to the new power relations? How had they been affected by the changes?

It is uncertain to what extent adults will ever be able to gain a comprehensive understanding of their generational relations with their own children, without focusing on those aspects that seem particularly relevant in the light of their own biographies or generation group's history. Their own involvement may restrict the realm of reflection on existing forms of behaviour and relationships between adults and children. In retrospect, it seems as if the war-children generation group tended to overlook certain aspects. They focused their attention on the tensions between dependence and autonomy, external control and personal development. What they did not consider, however, was whether these issues were perhaps of less importance to their children. Although intergenerational power relations had in no way been evened out, they had become depersonalised in the wake of the 1960s push of modernisation, and children and adults were equally affected by the structural constraints that were increasingly defining everyday life. Because the parents had been successful in their struggle to overcome the generational authority conflict, their children no longer had to struggle on this issue. Indeed, Mannheim drew attention to the fact that:

> ... any two generations following one another always fight different opponents, both within and without. While the older people may still be combating something in themselves or in the external world in such fashion that all their feelings and efforts and even their concepts and categories of thought are determined by that adversary, for the younger people this adversary may be simply non-existent: their primary orientation is an entirely different one.
>
> (Mannheim 1952 [1928]: 298–9)

What was 'entirely different' for the children of the war children? Assuming that these children really did constitute a 'generational unit', which aspects of inter-generational relations were particularly precarious in their lives? Were there other factors with the potential to influence the formation of a new generation group?

It might be easier to find an answer to these questions from today's perspective. I will attempt to do so with reference to the mother-child relationship, which is expressed in the division of labour in everyday family life.[2] When the women of the war-children generation group rebelled as young adults against the authority that their fathers began to reclaim after the war, their protests took the form of a rebellion against the male-dominated society. They wanted to participate in the world of work, and no longer valued the work of the housewife (Rerrich 1988). Nevertheless, from the 1970s the labour force participation of women with children in need of care increased only slowly in West Germany, and primarily in the form of part-time work. In practice, the majority of women continued to bear almost all of the responsibility for domestic labour. In the field of conflict between their demands for emancipation and the reality of life as a housewife, the changing conditions of childhood provided a way of enhancing the status of domestic labour, since emphasis on learning and socialisation in the new childhood concepts was accompanied by a redefinition of maternal duties. Mothers were held more accountable than ever for their children's development, socialisation and school achievement, and changes in the institutional and urban environment made it necessary for mothers to shape and organise their children's daily lives in a learning-directed manner. Many middle-class mothers readily assumed this challenging task, and pursued their children's advancement in a semi-professional manner by investing a great deal of time and effort in this undertaking, based on firm convictions and following the latest scientific trends. For many of these mothers from the war-children generation group – who prompted a complete rethink in the way adults interacted with children – the desire to do everything right, as well as in accordance with theories propagated by professional educationalists, often led to uncertainty in their dealings with children. Many of these mothers were also concerned by the contradictions implied in the spread of education to all domains of children's life – the contradiction between the goal of autonomy on the one hand, and the reality of more structural control on the other. On the one hand, the goal of rearing their children to independence corresponded with the mothers' desire for their children to grow up free from the authoritarian oppression that they themselves had suffered as children, as well as with their own aspirations to independence. Indeed, in the 1980s it was said that 'independent mothers need independent children' (Rauschenberg 1990). On the other hand, the need to foster children's learning and development meant that children became so central to family life that the family largely became a service provider for children. This brought mothers into a conflict between their emancipatory self-image and the reality of their role as attendants to their children's needs.

What position did children occupy in such family situations? Presumably, children will have perceived the ambivalence between expectations and reality in the way this was expressed in their mothers' behaviour: a conflict between calls for self-determination and independence on the one hand, and the constant surrounding of children with care and attention in the family context on the other. One domain in which this trend in generational relations can be seen particularly clearly is that of children's participation in domestic labour (Zeiher 2000; 2001b). In middle-class households such as those described above, the goal of fostering children's learning and development was generally so dominant that children were practically excluded from helping out at home – with the exception of the small chores they were allocated with the explicit aim of teaching them responsibility (cf Zelizer 1985). This can be regarded as a further step in the historical process by which children have been excluded from productive labour, a process that began with the state enforcement of compulsory school attendance, and has now spread rather successfully to the private household, a development which has also benefited children's schoolwork. Children seemed to receive constant attention without participating actively in domestic labour. Children were dependent on their parents' working to support and care for them, and at the same time they were expected to act autonomously – and independently of their parents.[3] Generally speaking, the social integration of children became precarious.

How did children respond to this ambivalent position in family life through their everyday activities? It seems unlikely that their experiences will have been unpleasant. Indeed, the children will barely have been consciously aware of them, as the personal relationships in which they were embedded were generally non-authoritarian and affectionate. In case studies conducted into the shaping of everyday life of ten-year-olds living in Berlin in the mid-1980s (Zeiher and Zeiher 1994), the conflict between independence and integration became apparent in diverse patterns of daily life and parent-child relationships. Illustrating this by comparing the patterns observed in individual families would go beyond the scope of this chapter. Instead, I would like to give an example from a domain of life in which the ten-year-olds were able to develop both aspects – independence and social integration – in their own way, namely social life with their peers outside of school in the afternoons (in Germany, most schools end at midday).

The Berlin girls and boys I discuss here lived in a middle-class district of Berlin, and all of them attended the same class at school. These children's afternoon meetings were organised in a network of twosomes, and they had developed rules to govern this. Children who wanted to spend the afternoon together would arrange to do so that morning at school. Back home for lunch, both of the children would discuss the plan with their mothers (or sometimes fathers) before telephoning to confirm the arrangement. Every meeting was thus preceded some hours earlier by goal-setting, anticipation, initiative and scheduling. No other children were allowed to join in with an arranged meeting, even good friends of the 'original' pair. The children changed their partners from one day to the next, preventing friendships from becoming too close or demands being made of each other, and, over the course of time, they had regular meetings with each partner to prevent the relationship petering out. Moreover, each relationship had to be organised in such a way that several relationships could exist side by side. This called for the conscious management of relationships: the children needed to make sure that they remained attractive to potential partners at the same time as keeping a balance between closeness and distance, such that individual relationships neither become too close nor died down. This type of arrangement ensured a social distance that gave each child the freedom to decide how to spend each new afternoon. Furthermore, the rules governing their social life meant that the children only had to commit themselves on the day in question, and not in the longer term. In other words, these children realised they needed to keep their temporal options open. The children used methods of rational organisation, namely time scheduling and regulation – structural forms of control that they had picked up in their care and educational institutions, as well as by observing their mothers' methods of time management – to maintain as much freedom as possible in making decisions on their peer relations. In so doing, they succeeded in achieving social integration without becoming too close to the other parties and making commitments that might have compromised their self-determination. They wanted friends, but they also wished to keep a certain distance. For short periods of time, this distance was repeatedly offset by the closeness that develops when spending the afternoon in pairs rather than in larger groups.

In jointly developing this form of social life and keeping to its rules, these children had, in their own way, responded to the problem underlying their family experiences, namely the ambivalence between independence and attachment, autonomy and belonging. These particular children managed to find a way of realising both of these qualities in their daily lives. In my opinion, this example may reveal a dominant theme determining the character of the generation group growing up in the 1970s and 1980s, namely the attempt to find a balance between independence and attachment.

The war children's grandchildren – are today's childhoods different again?

Let me now turn to the children of the present day. Again, this means looking first at the particular generation group their parents belong to. The children I have just described – the war children's children – are now themselves young parents. How are generational relations constructed within their families? How do they relate to their own children in the light of their own childhood experiences? In Germany, a number of recent studies have provided insights into the life plans and attitudes of today's young women (Geissler and Oechsle 1996; Blättel-Mink *et al.* 1998; Pasquale 1998). It emerges that those who already have children or intend to do so differ from their own mothers in a fundamental respect. Today's young women are said to want to have it all: a career, children, a partner, and equally the freedom to pursue their own personal interests. They aspire to self-determination and independence, but also want to be integrated in relationships with their partner and children. And indeed, it appears that many of them may succeed. Unlike their mothers, they no longer need to fight for their own emancipation. Nor do they need to find and implement an alternative to the childhood structures they experienced in their own youth – on either a general or a personal level. As a result of this, they seem to have a less ideological and more pragmatic approach to the care and rearing of children than their own mothers once did. While they want to provide their children with the best possible opportunities, and are willing to go to great lengths to achieve this, they are no longer prepared to subordinate their own autonomy to the autonomy of their children. Despite close bonds to their children and a firm commitment to the well-being and development of their children, these mothers aim to maintain their independence. Recent criticism of the central position the child occupies in the family, as well as the one-sidedness of the goal of self-determination, may well be a symptom of this. This criticism is a popular topic in the media, and bookshops stock self-help guides for parents with titles such as *Your Child, the Little Tyrant* and *The Child-Rearing Catastrophe: We need strong parents* (Hungerland 2003).

It might be possible to trace these characteristics and attitudes back to the specific childhood experiences of today's young adults in the way that I have attempted here. But in what kind of situations do such attitudes currently operate? How will such factors affect the generational relationships between these adults and their children? At this point, it is possible only to suggest a few tentative answers, extending the historical description given in this chapter. The parents of today's parents, the war-children generation group, improved the conditions for the development of their children's autonomy and intensified the societal segregation of children by means of increased institutionalisation. This societal project reached its climax and created a crisis in parent-child relationships of the 1980s. Since the 1990s, the self-determination of children has no longer simply been a child-rearing objective affecting the personal relationships between adults and children. Rather, it has left the confines of the pedagogical sphere and become established as legal principle. Children are now regarded as a sector of the population with rights to political participation and welfare. The tendency to segregate children, confining them to the protective and preparatory spheres of the family and the educational system, has begun to be broken down at the societal level. Firstly, consumer markets and the media are becoming more important in children's lives, and it is in precisely these areas that children are treated as full members of society (Hengst 1996). Secondly, some borders of the child-specific worlds are being eroded – the borders between the world of work and the world of childhood, for example, which were formerly constitutive of the differentiation of childhood in modern society. Schoolchildren with weekend or evening jobs are breaking down these boundaries. Studies conducted in several European countries have shown that children not only work in order to gain a measure of economic independence, but that they explicitly seek to participate in 'real life' and take on responsibility (Hengst and Zeiher 2000; Mizen *et al.* 2001). In sum, it can be concluded that children's participation and integration were the main features of the changing socio-structural conditions in the 1990s; nowadays the theme of control, which was so important in previous decades, seems to be replaced by that of integration.

The extent to which families are actually affected by such changes has to be a research issue, as is the nature of the generational relations jointly produced in everyday family life by today's parents and their children. The position children occupy within the family is undergoing change, partly because increasing numbers of mothers now work, but primarily because of the recent increase in flexible and irregular working hours. This makes it necessary for childcare to be redistributed between families and external organisations. It may also be the case that new divisions of labour are required within the family, with children again being expected to help out more at home, for example. Which experiences are precarious for children in these new circumstances? Will children of a new generation group emerge in the wake of the current economic and temporal upheavals, and what might be their central theme? It is too early for answers to these questions. In this chapter, I can only call for questions such as these to be considered, and for future research and reflection to take account of the specific historical experiences of the generation of adults with whom these children interact.

In this chapter, I have tried to argue for the advantages of approaching analyses of intergenerational relationships from the Mannheimian perspective of historical generations. This argument has been rather tentative. At its conclusion, I would like to draw attention to the fact that the examples given are restricted in at least three ways. Firstly, they are confined to middle-class families in West Germany. Secondly, only one particular succession of generation groups was considered. Although the birth cohorts who were children during the Second World War, in the period of the 'push of modernisation' and in the current period of post-modernity obviously experienced very different childhoods, this cannot be regarded as a full image of generations in recent childhood history. Thirdly, corresponding to particular events in history, certain successive birth cohorts may form generation groups (in Mannheim's sense). However, what I have done here, namely allocating a particular generation group of parents to children of a particular generation group, is rather artificial because of the broad range of birth cohorts becoming parents at any one time.

Notes

1 In this chapter, the term 'generation group' is used in order to distinguish between generation as a group of people born at about the same time and characterised by common experiences and consciousness of a common identity (in the sense of Mannheim) from 'generation' as a social category or structure in the generational order of a society (a childhood generation opposing an adult generation at a time).

2 Since Karl Mannheim, historical generations (generation groups) have primarily been defined in terms of differences in their political experiences and conflicts

with their fathers. This corresponds to the distribution of roles in bourgeois society; fathers were responsible for politics and society, and for making their power felt by the upcoming generation group. The members of the 1980 working group also traced the particularities of their own generation group back to their fathers – more specifically, to their absence during the war and their subsequent return. Since then, bourgeois gender relations have been broken down, and it is no longer appropriate to perceive societal and political change in purely patriarchal terms.

3 When children of this generation group reached adolescence, the ambivalence of their mothers' behaviour and expectations – keeping a firm hold on their children while expecting them to become independent and leave home – was expressed in the public discussion about what became known as children using the 'Hotel Mama'.

References

Blättel-Mink, B., Kramer, C. and Mischau, A. (1998) *Lebensalltag von Frauen zwischen Tradition und Moderne*. Baden-Baden: Nomos.

du Bois-Reymond, M, Büchner, P., Krüger, H.-H., Ecarius, J. and Fuhs, B. (1994) 'Die moderne Familie als Verhandlungshaushalt'. In M. du Bois-Reymond *et al.*, *Kinderleben. Modernisierung von Kindheit im interkulturellen Vergleich*. Opladen: Leske and Budrich.

Büchner, P. (1983) 'Vom Befehlen und Gehorchen zum Verhandeln'. In U. Preuss-Lausitz, P. Büchner, M. Fischer-Kowalski, D. Geulen, M.E. Karsten, C. Kulke, U. Rabe-Kleberg, H.-G. Rolff, B. Thunemeyer, Y. Schütze, P. Seidl, H. Zeiher, and P. Zimmermann (eds), *Kriegskinder, Konsumkinder, Krisenkinder*. Weinheim and Basel: Beltz.

Bude, H. (2000) 'Die biographische Relevanz der Generation'. In M. Kohli and M. Sydlik (eds), *Generationen in Familie und Gesellschaft*. Opladen: Leske and Budrich.

Ecarius, J. (ed) (1998) *Was will die jüngere mit der älteren Generation? Generationsbeziehungen und Generationenverhältnisse in der Erziehungswissenschaft*. Opladen: Leske and Budrich.

Elder, G.H. (1974) *Children of the Great Depression*. Chicago: University of Chicago Press.

Elder, G.H. and Caspi, A. (1991) 'Lebensverläufe im Wandel der Gesellschaft: Soziologische und psychologische Perspektiven'. In A. Engfer, B. Minsel and S. Walper (eds), *Zeit für Kinder! Kinder in Familie und Gesellschaft*. Weinheim and Basel: Beltz.

Geissler, B. and Oechsle, M. (1996) *Lebensplanung junger Frauen. Zur widersprüchlichen Modernisierung weiblicher Lebensläufe.* Weinheim: Deutscher Studienverlag.

Hengst, H. (1996) 'Kinder an die Macht! Der Rückzug des Marktes aus dem Kindheitsprojekt der Moderne'. In H. Zeiher, P. Büchner and J. Zinnecker (eds), *Kinder als Außenseiter? Umbrüche in der gesellschaftlichern Wahrnehmung von Kindern und Kindheit.* Weinheim and München: Juventa.

Hengst, H. and Zeiher, H. (eds) (2000) *Die Arbeit der Kinder. Kindheitskonzept und Arbeitsteilung zwischen den Generationen.* Weinheim and München: Juventa.

Hungerland, B. (2003) '"Und so gedeiht das Baby". Altersgerechte Entwicklung und Gesundheit als gesellschaftliche Norm und Leistung'. In H. Hengst and H. Kelle (eds), *Kinder, Körper, Identitäten.* Weinheim and München: Juventa.

Kirchhöfer, D. (1998) *Aufwachsen in Ostdeutschland.* Weinheim and München: Juventa.

Liebau, E. and Wulf, C. (eds) (1996) *Generation. Versuche über eine pädagogischanthropologische Grundbedingung.* Weinheim: Deutscher Studienverlag.

Lüscher, K. and Schultheis, F. (eds) (1993) *Generationenbeziehungen in "postmodernen" Gesellschaften.* Konstanz: Universitätsverlag.

Mannheim, K. (1952 [1928]) 'The problem of generations'. In K. Mannheim (ed), *Essays on the Sociology of Knowledge.* London: Routledge and Kegan Paul.

Mansel, J., Rosenthal, G. and Tölke, A. (eds) (1997) *Generationenbeziehungen, Austausch und Tradierung.* Opladen: Westdeutscher Verlag.

Mizen, P., Pole, C. and Bolton, A. (eds) (2001) *Hidden Hands: International perspectives on children's work and labour.* London: RoutledgeFalmer.

Pasquale, J. (1998) *Die Arbeit der Mütter. Verberuflichung und Professionalisierung moderner Mutterarbeit.* Weinheim and München: Juventa.

Preuss-Lausitz, U., Büchner, P., Fischer-Kowalski, M., Geulen, D., Karsten, M.E., Kulke, C., Rabe-Kleberg, U., Rolff, H.-G., Thunemeyer, B., Schütze, Y., Seidl, P., Zeiher, H. and Zimmermann P. (1983) *Kriegskinder, Konsumkinder, Krisenkinder. Zur Sozialisationsgeschichte seit dem Zweiten Weltkrieg.* Weinheim and Basel: Beltz.

Preuss-Lausitz, U., Rülcker, T. and Zeiher, H. (eds) (1990) *Selbständigkeit für Kinder–die große Freiheit?* Weinheim and Basel: Beltz.

Rauschenberg, B. (1990) 'Hänschen klein ging allein ... Wege in die Selbständigkeit'. In U. Preuss-Lausitz, T. Rülcker and H. Zeiher (eds), *Selbständigkeit für Kinder – die große Freiheit?* Weinheim and Basel: Beltz.

Rerrich, M.S. (1988) *Balanceakt Familie. Zwischen alten Leitbildern und neuen Lebensformen.* Freiburg: Lambertus.

Rosenthal, G. (1997) 'Zur interaktionellen Konstitution von Generationen'. In J. Mansel, G. Rosenthal and A. Tölke (eds), *Generationen-Beziehungen, Austausch und Tradierung.* Opladen: Westdeutscher Verlag.

Uhle, R. (1996) 'Über die Verwendung des Generationen-Konzepts in der These von der 89er Generation'. In E. Liebau and C. Wulf (eds), *Generation. Über eine pädagogisch-anthropologische Grundbedingung*. Weinheim: Deutscher Studienverlag.

Zeiher, H. (2000) 'Hausarbeit: zur Integration der Kinder in die häusliche Arbeitsteilung'. In H. Hengst and H. Zeiher (eds), *Die Arbeit der Kinder. Kindheitskonzept und Arbeitsteilung zwischen den Generationen*. Weinheim and München: Juventa.

— (2001a) 'Children's islands in space and time: the impact of spatial differentiation on children's ways of shaping social life'. In M. du Bois-Reymond, H. Sünker and H.-H. Krüger (eds), *Childhood in Europe. Approaches – trends – findings*. New York: Peter Lang.

— (2001b) 'Dependent, independent and interdependent relations: children as members of the family household in West Berlin'. In L. Alanen and B. Mayall (eds), *Conceptualizing child-adult relations*. London and New York: Routledge-Falmer.

Zeiher, H.J. and Zeiher, H. (1994) *Orte und Zeiten der Kinder: Soziales Leben im Alltag von Großstadtkindern*. Weinheim and München: Juventa.

Zelizer, V.A. (1985) *Pricing the Priceless Child: The changing social value of children*. New York: Basic Books.